Long Term Deflation

Secret tips to Investing in Gov.Bonds for Economic Freedom

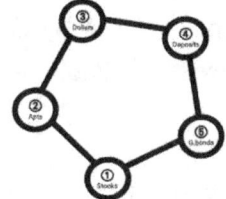

Copyright Notice

Long Term Deflation

Secret tips to Investing in Gov.Bonds for Economic Freedom

Subtitle:: **Jackpot secret** : How to invest in gov. bond

**Copyright (c)2024 by Sohn DaeShig.
All right reserved.** Published by Sohn DaeShig,

ISBN:979-11-392-1856-5(paperback)
ISBN:979-11-392-1857-2(hard cover)
ISBN:979-11-392-1858-9 (eBOOK)

All right reserved. No parts of this publication may be republished,distributed,or transmitted in any form or by any means including photographing, recording or other electronic or mechanical methods without the prior written permission of the publisher and auther,except in the case of brief quotations embodied in critical reviews and certain other non commercial uses permitted by copyright law.

Contact Information: sohn2738@naver.com

About the author(Korean):

The author was born in 1953. He was born during the Korean War and has experienced Korea's political, economic, social, and cultural development from the 1960s, when Korea was at its most difficult, to the present, when Korea has entered the developed world. He has been investing in stocks and apartments for more than 50 years.

In September 2011, after fulfilling his duties as a PD specializing in current & cultural affairs at KBS public broadcaster in korea for 30 years, he began to write financial(fintech) books professionally by gathering his own investment experience and the materials he researched in his spare time. He has written about seven books on financial technology. He is a licensed broker and has completed the CRO course.

Bibliographies: Author Sohn DaeShig's main books

1) Jan. 2, 2018. (A financial secret handbook that only passes on to children, 390pages) Korean Edition
2) Apr. 2, 2018. (Tears of the Japanese, 261pages) Korean Edition
3) Mar. 22, 2019. (Rent investors are stupid investors, 371pages) Korean Edition
4) Aug. 10, 2021. (The Fall of Wealth, 298pages) Korean Edition
5) Dec. 1, 2021. (Tears of Korean, 424pages) Korean Edition
6) Sep. 1, 2023. (Wealth Creation, The Hidden Story, 99pages) (How to start investing at age 60 and succeed) Korean Edition
7) March 4,2024(Dollar Swap Fintech Make 800% Assets Market rotation investing Formula.Pentagon Investing Method, 374 pages)Korean & English Edition

Prologue

Long term deflation will cause all asset prices to collapse by 80-90%, so it's a golden opportunity to go from laborer to capitalist, from nothing to get rich, as long as you prepare ahead of time.

The Long Term Deflation is a war of survival: get rich or get wiped out. Very little economic data from 1929 remains for the United States. Japan's data from 1990~2023 is the only one worth analyzing and studying. Even globally, there is very little data on long term deflation, let alone the usual short term deflation line.

Japan's long term deflation data and so on, are thankfully updated and published monthly by FRED. It was a great pleasure for the author to be able to cite these sources to verify almost all of his arguments.

This book is the first general theory of long term deflation. In a nutshell, long term deflation is a proportional decline in the price of the dollar and the price of everything else in the world over a period of 5 to 30 years.

According to the author's diamond dollar investment method, the dollar and the price of goods should be inversely proportional. However, the opposite phenomenon occurs: a direct relationship between the dollar and the price of everything in the world, lasting 5~30 years.

If we analyze Japan in December 1988, the domestic dollar price and the Nikkei 225 stock price rose about 30% in proportion for about a year. It was a sign of the beginning of long term deflation.

Now, in South Korea, the domestic price of the dollar and the domestic stock market are surging.

The U.S. Great Depression of 1929 was the world's first long term deflation, and Japan's in 1989 lasted 32 years. In a long term deflation, the price of everything in the world, and the dollar, is constantly falling, so there is almost nothing to invest in, and the only asset that can be invested in is government bonds, which we will discuss in detail in this book.

This book is the first book to focus on this phenomenon of long term deflation, and it emphasizes why deflation should be divided into short term and long term deflation, and how these two types of deflation differ.

This book is not a research book or an economics text, but an investment theory book, and summarizes the results of research on long term deflation to be used as an investment method as much as possible. I have already announced that there is an investment order among the top five assets in the asset market.

It involves rotating through five assets: stocks, apartments, dollars, deposits, and government bonds. This is what the authors call the pentagon asset cycle investing method because it's a pentagonal shape.

The final stage of this asset allocation cycle is to invest in government bonds. While a normal long term deflation is over in two to three years, a long term deflation usually lasts about 5~30 years. During this period, stocks, apartments, the dollar, gold, and everything else in the world crashes for a very long time.

In this business cycle, we've gone from stocks, to apartments, to dollar swaps, to deposits, and then to a situation where we had to put all our money in government bonds to survive.

The global long term deflation that began in 2016 is expected to run through 2043, with brief periods of inflation in the form of the 2006 subprime crisis, the 2020 coronavirus pandemic, and the increase in excess money supply.

Once inflation has subsided, the world must now fight a long, long battle against deflation.

When Long Term Deflation arrives,
Prices of all goods collapse for 30 years.
The dollar's exchange rate crashes.
In response, stocks, apartments, dollars, and everything else drop by 80-90%.
Gold also falls.
Bitcoin and other virtual assets also crash.
So, it's a long term deflation where anyone who holds anything valuable for a long period of time will be ruined.

Therefore, the author focuses on the all-encompassing question: In a long term deflation, how will I survive? How can I capitalize on the downfall of wealth to get rich?

In a long term deflation, you should only invest in assets that go up, and that is government bonds. This book gives you the opportunity to capitalize on this deflation and get rich.

The long term deflation in the U.S. and Japan shows that no country has a solution, and neither do the world's leading scholars. This is the first long term deflation that has reached the entire world. Hyperinflation, moderate inflation, short term deflation, etc. can be controlled by the government's will, but long term deflation cannot be controlled, so there is no real solution.

We'll have a chance to look at this in more detail. If you look at Japan's long-run deflation, which started in

1989, they were the best off country at the time, and suddenly they had a long-run deflation because of the exchange rate surge.

One of the best performing countries in the world since the 1980s is South Korea. South Korea has weathered all the crises and continued to grow, so the impact of an unprecedented Long Term Deflation would be much more psychological and physical than in other countries. The causes of a long term deflation can vary from country to country, and there are many, but we already know that the common demographic problem will not be solved in 30 years, as in Japan.

The author's arguments are all supported by FRED's graphs. I hope that by reading this book, every individual investor will go beyond How Will I Survive, and become a successful investor.

The author would like to thank FRED and Microsoft for providing the analysis. To the best of my knowledge, this is the first time the author has attempted a full-scale study and review of long term deflation using these resources. I hope that this book will create an atmosphere to study long term deflation.

2024.5.15.

Pangyo in Korea.

Table of Contents

Prologue

(Part One)

The Fall of Riches

Chapter 1) Long Term Deflation and Short Term Deflation

Chapter 2) Why distinguish between short and long term deflation?

Chapter 3) The fall of riches:Your riches will fall like America's and Japan's.

Chapter 4) Causes of Long Term Deflation(1) Dollar Weakness

Chapter 5) Is South Korea's foreign exchange reserve adequate for a so-called dollar ATM country?

Chapter 6) High vs. low US dollar exchange rate policies

Chapter 7) Causes of Long Term Deflation(2) -Population decline

Chapter 8) Causes of Long Term Deflation(3)Overindebtedness

Chapter 9) Catching the Deflationary Moment

-In individual countries

Chapter 10) Catching the Deflationary Moment

-In the world

Chapter 11) Neither Korea nor the world can escape Japanese-style long term deflation.

(Part Two)

Long Term Deflation Is a Complete Jackpot Opportunity

Chapter 12) Investing in a Long Term Deflation

Chapter 13) Best: Only Invest in Gov. Bonds During Step 5

Chapter 14) Second Best: Short stocks.apartments too

Chapter 15) New Asset Allocation method (Diamond dollar dichotomy method) The diamond dollar dichotomy doesn't work in long term deflation

Chapter 16) If it becomes long term deflation dollar, stocks and real estate collapses

Chapter 17) If it becomes long term deflation bitcoin and gold will collapse too!

(Part Three)

Japan is no longer a Long Term Deflation country

Chapter 18) Long term deflation of the Japan i.e,Japan's Collapse and Revive... and Beyond

Chapter 19) When will the inflation economy come back?

Epilogue

(Part One)
The Fall of Riches

In an inflationary economy, even if you borrowed money from the bank, bought real things such as real estate and kept them, or just kept the real estate you received as an inheritance, you got rich automatically because of the continuous increase in prices.

As the inflationary economy continued for about 70 years before and after World War II, the stereotype that you can get rich by not selling real estate or stocks was developed. The so-called land myth was born and the idea that anyone can get rich by investing in stocks or real estate for the long term.

But in short term deflation, which is what we've been experiencing, the price of everything goes down. In every short term deflation, the dollar surges for a year or two and the prices of apartments, stocks, commodities, etc. fall accordingly.

In a long term deflation, unlike a short term deflation, i.e. a normal recession, the dollar collapses and prices of apartments, stocks, commodities, etc. collapse. Interest rates also converge to 0%. All asset prices collapse simultaneously, so the number of investment means becomes extremely small.

In other words, all assets will almost certainly crash, making conventional investing the perfect contrarian investment.

In deflation, whether it's short or long term, everything in the world becomes less valuable over time, especially real estate and stocks, which continue to decline in value. As a result, wealth has shifted to cash holders. In other words, the relative prices of assets change.

Eventually, the wealth of those who didn't react falls, as does all the wealth in the world.

The reason why the fall of riches is spontaneous is that in deflation, real prices are constantly falling.
On the other hand, the value of cash is comparatively the same as the value of all goods because the prices of all goods are falling. This is because wealth that grew by holding onto it during inflation becomes worth less the longer you hold onto it during deflation.

It is estimated that Korea will not be out of the deep long term deflation until about 2029 and all other countries until 2048. This book provides an opportunity to explore the reasons and specific phenomena.

In deflationary times, those who have real estate and other tangible things don't get rich, they get destroyed.

Logically explain why renting, gap investing, stock investing, overseas investing, and gold investing are all bad investments. Compare and verify this with 48 years of surging Japanese yen, Nikkei index, and crashing Japanese housing index.

If you look at the Great Depression in the United States in 1929, and Japan in 1989, and learn how to invest in a long term deflation in advance and prepare for it, you can go from being a salaryman to getting 10x or even 100x richer.

It's the first opportunity in 70 years to move up the ladder from laborer to capitalist. But for those who are not prepared for long term deflation, it is not an opportunity, but the dreaded "D".

Chapter 1)

Long Term Deflation and Short Term Deflation

When you see the title of this book, your first reaction is probably to gasp and laugh before you even start reading. This is because right now, the world is not in deflation, but rather in hyperinflation, having just come off a massive interest rate hike of about 2500% (0.25%->5.25%).

However, the real fear, Long Term Deflation, has already started in January 2016. Let's take a look at the difference between the effects of short term deflation, which is what we're usually used to, and the effects of long term deflation, which is what we're used to during a normal recession, so that we can summarize future measures and investment tips.

First, let's define long term deflation. The difference between a long term deflation in a country and a long term deflation internationally starts with the concept.

Long term deflation in a country is defined as a phenomenon in which the domestic dollar price, domestic stock index, and all commodity prices fall proportionally for about 5~30 years.

The global long term deflation is a phenomenon where the international dollar price, the dollar index price, and the international gold price fall together for about 5~30 years, and of course, international commodity prices also fall proportionally. No one has experienced a global long term deflation yet.

As you can see, short term deflation and long term deflation are completely different phenomena in the asset markets, and the investment approach should be completely different. That's why it's important to distinguish between the two types of deflation. So, how do you distinguish between them?

Short term deflation is defined by the duration of the deflation, which is no longer than five years. This is because one business cycle is usually five years of good times and five years of bad times. After Keynesian economics, the government's ability to regulate the economy has increased, so it is more common for a single business cycle to be shorter than 10 years.

However, there is a huge difference in the duration of deflation, with the U.S. Great Depression of 1929 lasting 22 years and Japan's 1989 deflation lasting a whopping 32 years. In a short term deflation, asset prices fall for a shorter period of time than in a long term deflation.

1) During the 1929 U.S. Long Depression, U.S. stocks would have fallen 87.1% and real estate would have fallen by a similar percentage.

2) In Japan in 1989, stocks fell by 80% and apartments by 90%.

In a short term deflation, the Diamond dollar investment method still applies, so as the dollar rises, all domestic assets, including stocks and real estate such as apartments, fall.

Secondly, we can distinguish between a straight diamond dollar investment or an inverse diamond dollar investment.

The Diamond Dollar Investing Method is an investment method that states that outside of the United States, the dollar and all commodities always move in opposite directions and should be invested accordingly. In contrast, when the dollar and the price of all goods move in the same direction and in proportion to each other, the inverse diamond dollar investing method is applied.

In a long term deflation, the inverse Diamond Dollar investment method is applied, so when the dollar price falls, stocks and apartments crash. Let's take a look at the Japanese example, which is illustrated in [Figure 2], which shows the evolution of the yen-dollar exchange rate, the Nikkei index, and the housing index over a 48-year period.

Schematically, before BC'②, we can see the three-factors relationship during short-term deflation, i.e., during normal economic conditions, the yen-dollar exchange rate graph at the top and the Nikkei index in the center have been rising sharply according to the Diamond Dollar Investment Method.

The vertical dotted line BC'② is where Japan's long term deflation began. The Ⓐ line is December 16, 2012, the day Abenomics was implemented.

The graph at the bottom shows the change in the Nikkei index and the Japanese housing index over a 48-year period, starting in February 1971, as the yen/dollar exchange rate changed from 357.56 yen.

If you draw a vertical dotted line anywhere, you can see the correlation between the yen/dollar exchange rate on that day and the corresponding Nikkei and house prices. To make it easier to compare the correlations, the author has intentionally rearranged the dates of the graphs provided by the FRB.

The bottom graph is the Japanese housing index for the same period, but it was not published before 2010 and has been published since around 2010, so it is a very convenient graph that shows the relationship between the yen-dollar exchange rate and the Nikkei index at a glance.

Long term deflation after BC'② As you can see from the graph in [Figure 2], the inverse relationship between the dollar and other commodities, i.e., the basic principle of the Diamond Dollar Investment Method, does not work at all when long term deflation occurs.

In short, long deflationary periods are not common sense investing times. These phenomena cannot be explained or solved by conventional economic theories. This is the phenomenon and theory of long term deflation that the author concludes by analyzing Japan.

In a short term deflation, the diamond dollar investment method causes the yen-dollar exchange rate and all goods to move in opposite directions. However, as shown in BC'② below, in a long deflation, the Diamond Dollar investment method that usually works well is reversed.

The investment method in a short deflationary period is completely opposite to the investment method in a long deflationary period. Therefore, Japan has shown that you can get rich by learning the consequences of a long deflationary period 30 years in advance and investing accordingly.

In the case of Japan, if the yen-dollar exchange rate and the price of all goods were determined according to the theory of short term deflation, which is a generalized recession, there should have been a huge surge in the price of stocks and apartments as the dollar fell and the yen rose according to the Diamond Dollar Investment Method.

But instead, the opposite happened: apartment prices crashed, stocks crashed, and the dollar crashed.

This is what makes long term deflation completely different from classical deflation. This is why economists and research centers have been unable to solve Japan's long term deflation for 30 years.

Deflation slowly reduces demand as all prices fall, reducing the amount of imports and thus the demand for dollars. Long term deflation reduces the price of consumer goods in the country, which in turn reduces the demand for dollars from imports. It also reduces demand for stocks and apartments. In Japan, this has been a recurring economic phenomenon for 30 years.

Now that Japan is out of long term deflation, this has changed somewhat, but Japanese money is still heading overseas. The reason for this is that there is nowhere to invest in Japan due to long term deflation. Since there is no profit in investing anywhere in Japan, it is seemingly more profitable to go overseas because of the yield itself. However, in the meantime, they are losing more money due to the depreciation of the dollar.

The this round of Long Term Deflation is already upon the world in January 2016. No one can escape it. Although the depth of deflation varies from country to country, this book explains in detail that Long Term Deflation has already arrived in Korea and around the world.

The goal of this book is not to be an academic study of long term deflation. That is for academics and researchers at economic research institutes, not for us investors.

The goal of this book is to guide investors, the readers of

this book, on the path to getting rich by analyzing the price movements of stocks, apartments, dollars, and government bonds during short term deflation or long term deflation, and by analyzing Japan's 30 years of long term deflation and investing against it.

In other words, the goal is to provide readers with the knowledge to get rich on the cheap, using Japanese analysis. In the end, it's all about survival and investing in a long term deflation.

This book is an opportunity to change from a family of workers to a family of capitalists, so I hope that you will study and prepare for the long term deflation in advance. We have experienced it many times, but if we don't study and prepare ourselves in advance, we will not be able to cope with the same situation.

January 4, 1990 marked the beginning of Japan's longest

deflation. Or, more precisely, in December 1988, about a year before that. This is the vertical dotted line BC'② in [Figure 2].

The relationship between the yen-dollar exchange rate and the Nikkei clearly indicates that Japan's long term deflation, or Great Recession as it is commonly known, had already started a year before.

However, no one knew this, and certainly no one invested accordingly, because it wasn't until decades later that the author ingeniously identified this period and defined it as a long term deflationary phenomenon.

Anyone who had invested accordingly, i.e. cashed out all their assets at this time, could have multiplied their wealth many times over in a short period of time. However, if he had not invested against the continued surge in the yen, i.e. against long term deflation, his stocks would have fallen by about 80% and his real estate by about 90% in 30 years. This is what happened to Japan and the Japanese people.

Unlike the recent wave of heavy investment in profitable assets in Korea, Japanese people haven't invested in any profitable assets since 30 years ago.
They don't even buy houses anymore. The reason is that if you buy a house as an investment or invest in a profitable asset for rent, you will lose money every year.

For example, if you get 20 million won a year in rent fee, but the price of a house drops by 30 million won a year for 30 years, doesn't it make sense not to buy a house? This happens over 30 years, not just a year or two. Who wants to buy a rental investment home when you're losing money every time you hold on to it?

The Japanese were once internationally known as the Economic Animals, so calculating and obsessed with money. However, one of the things they learned after more than 30 years of doing nothing but stupid things, starting with the Great Japanese Crash of 1990, is that investing in real estate, especially rental properties, is a losing proposition.

Buying an investment home, or even a home to live in, is an investment that you can only make if you're willing to take a big loss because home prices have been falling for 30 years.

Therefore, the land myth, which is still believed in by Koreans in almost similar economic conditions, has long since disappeared in Japan. However, Japanese families have fewer children, so they are forced to inherit one house from each side of the parents, resulting in one or two additional houses per family. In order to reduce property taxes on inherited houses, people are now bulldozing them to make way for new houses.

Considering the current real estate market in Korea, you might think that it would be nice to inherit one or two apartments from both families, so that you can live in your own house and rent out the inherited house. However, since everyone has one or two apartments in addition to their current home, there is no one to pay the rent. This is the current state of the Japanese housing market and the future of the Korean housing market and apartment market.

In addition, Japanese people have been investing only in foreign stocks due to a 32-year long deflation. The subsequent strengthening of the yen has turned the money into ghost dollars that can't even be brought back into the country. The Watanabe women, who went abroad at the recommendation of their securities brokers, have been dying for more than 30 years.

As a result, Japanese people had nowhere to invest their money, neither in Japan nor abroad. Interest rates on bank deposits and bank loans in Japan are around 0%. Interest on government bonds is also negative, and there are no government bonds for sale.

Where would you invest your money if there was no profit to be made?
Put it in a closet or deposit it in a bank, the result is the same. Abenomics helicoptered money into Japan in 2020 and solved the country's long term deflation.

It's a kind of rite of passage in a long deflation period. There is also the myth that Japanese people don't buy houses because of the earthquake. That's not true. It is human greed, the providence of money, and the motive of profit-seeking that makes people buy houses come hell or high water, not earthquakes. They don't buy because there is no profit.

Everyone needs a house to live in, but the more you have, the worse it is, so you don't buy a house. As the term "economic animal" suggests, the Japanese are extremely wise.

Historically, every decade in the business cycle, there has been a short term deflationary decline in asset values due to the bursting of bubbles. However, while they soon normalized within two to three years after the collapse, this time around, the long term deflation will be a deflation that will last for five to 30 years.

Identifying long term deflation is surprisingly simple. Of course, the author's method of identifying evidence is unique to his research. If you believe that a long term deflation is coming, you should check the evidence and reverse your investments.

That's the only way to survive. The world, with the exception of Japan, has been in a state of long term deflation since 2016. The 2008 financial crisis and the 2020 coronavirus pandemic briefly triggered inflation with loose money, but the long term deflation is now in full swing.

Chapter 2)

Why distinguish between short and longer term deflation?

As I mentioned in the previous chapter, different types of deflation require 180 degree changes in how you invest, which means you'll be completely screwed if you don't invest differently. So, the first thing you need to do is to categorize deflation into long and short deflation.

When prices fall and the economy stagnates, it is called deflation. A typical business cycle consists of booms and busts, i.e., five years of inflation and five years of deflation.

The duration of a full-blown inflationary or deflationary period is estimated to be about three years each. In the

U.S., a recession, or short term deflation, or simply deflation, occurs when GDP grows negatively for two consecutive quarters. However, a typical deflation is a period of falling prices and economic stagnation for up to five years.

On the other hand, there are also long deflation periods, such as 22 years in the U.S. or 32 years in Japan, which the authors define as long term deflation and analyze and explain separately from short term deflation.

Investing in a short term deflation has not changed much, except for the addition of DollarSwap and government bonds. However, it is important to remember that outside of the US, the process of swapping assets into dollars is mandatory.

In other words, outside of the U.S., the fact that you have to go through the process of swapping dollars is very different from traditional financial technology, or fintech, methods. This dollar swap transaction is the core theory of the Pentagon investing method advocated by the author,

The author's formula for asset market rotation is that investors should rotate their money in the following order: ① stocks → ② apartments → ③ dollars → ④ deposits → ⑤ government bonds. The theory is that everyone should rotate their investments in this order because it will yield the greatest return. The author named this five-step rotation method as the Pentagon investing method.

Investing without following this five-step investment sequence is called reverse investment. Just like a big accident can happen if you drive backwards, reversing the order of circular investments or investing backwards can cause a big accident by increasing the amount of losses.

By rotating all assets into dollars in three stages, you can achieve a return of about 4x (up to 8x) in a short period of time, which is the Diamond Dollar Investment Method.

When investing in asset markets such as real estate and stocks in Korea during a short-term deflation, i.e., during a normal recession, you should understand how to invest by looking at the process of finding a balance between the dollar and assets through the process of bubbles and counter-bubbles.

Since the price of dollars and the price of assets are inversely related, you must always fund, invest, or redeem dollars or assets in a diamond shape.

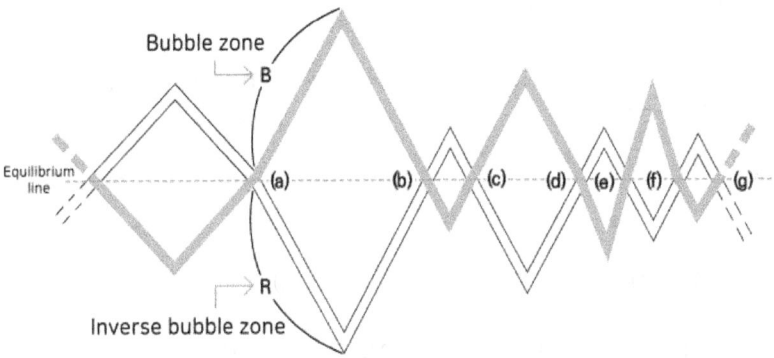

[Fig.1] Understanding the Diamond dollar investment method during a short-term deflation: The process of finding a balance between dollars and assets through bubbles and counter-bubbles.

The horizontal line in the center of [Figure 1] is the equilibrium between the dollar and assets (stocks, apartments, gold, crude oil, copper, etc.). After the equilibrium price is disrupted by the financial crisis etc., the equilibrium price of the dollar and the price of the asset will find its equilibrium point through numerous bubbles and counter-bubbles.

In [Figure 1], the black line represents the movement of the dollar, and the white line represents the movement of goods such as apartments, stocks, gold, etc. whose prices change in response to the movement of the dollar.

As in the first diamond, if for some reason the equilibrium is disturbed and the dollar starts to fall, then apartments, stocks, goods, etc. will rise proportionally.

After that, the dollar and commodity prices temporarily find equilibrium, but then, for whatever reason, the dollar rises significantly and the prices of apartments, stocks, and commodities fall inversely in proportion to the dollar's rise, which is the second diamond shape.

In this way, commodity prices repeat large and small diamond shapes in response to the movement of the dollar, and the bubble (B) and reverse bubble (R) between the dollar and commodity prices eventually dissolve and find an equilibrium point.

This process of bubbles and counter-bubbles will eventually lead to a fair price for apartments, stocks, and other goods that corresponds to the price of the dollar in normal times without financial crises.

Eventually, the price of all goods will be inversely related to the dollar, and when the dollar price becomes insignificant, the price of goods will fluctuate very little with the dollar price, and only the supply and demand factor will remain.

With the exception of those who live in the United States and use the dollar as their everyday currency, all wealth in this world must be invested and withdrawn in reverse to match the rise or fall of the dollar.

The Diamond Dollar Investment Method is an investment method that invests in all goods such as stocks and apartments during short term deflation. If you follow this method in the long term deflation, you will completely fail. Therefore, you need to categorize deflation as short term or long term deflation.

[Figure 2] is a graph that analyzes the relationship between the Japanese yen-dollar exchange rate and the Nikkei and Japanese real estate prices over a period of about 48 years.

Again, by looking vertically below and above any vertical dotted line, you can compare the simultaneous or bi-directional changes in the yen-dollar exchange rate, the Nikkei index, and Japanese house prices in the same year and month.

So you can see and understand how to invest in a short term deflation period and how to invest in a long term deflation period at the same time.

48 years is a long time, so you can learn how to invest in the inflation period and how to invest in the long deflation period all in one graph.

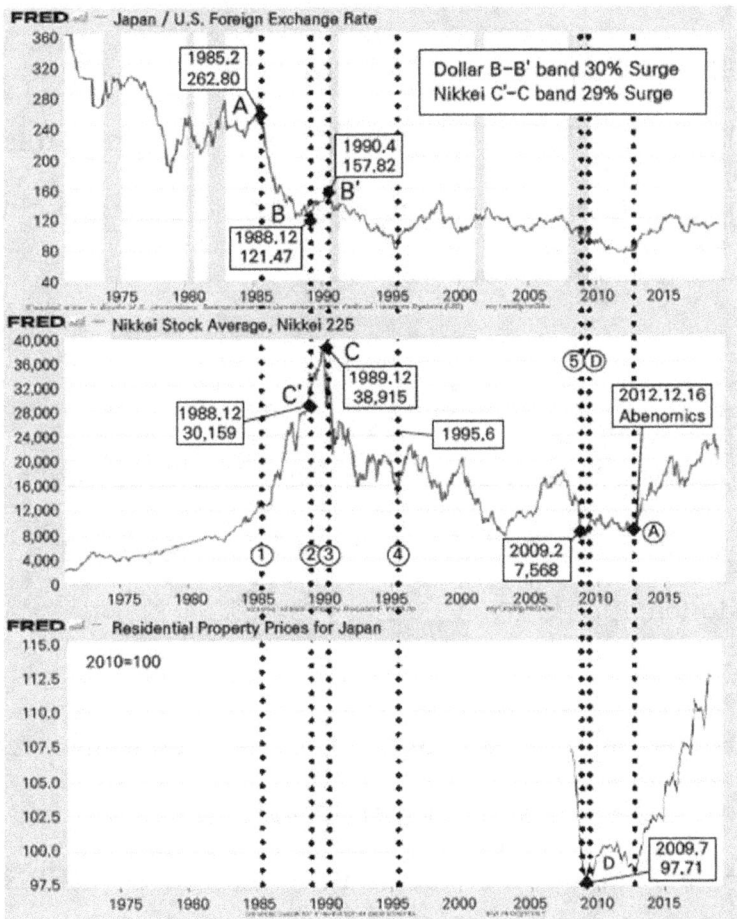

[Fig.2] 48 year change in the price of the yen and the Nikkei and housing indices

Now, let's take a closer look at the three-way relationship between deflation, short term deflation, and long term deflation.

First, let's look at the vertical dotted line ①, which is February 1985. The market price of the yen at this time is 262.80 yen. This means that it costs 262.80 yen to buy one dollar.

After the Plaza Agreement in September 1985, the yen continued to rise, and by June 1995, the dollar had reached the bottom. This is the time of the vertical dotted line ④.

By December 1988, point B, the yen continues to rise, reaching 121.47 yen per dollar. That's a staggering 53.6% jump in the yen. You can see in the middle graph of the Nikkei Stock Average that the Nikkei has risen sharply in proportion to the yen's rise.

While it is commonly believed that a rising yen-dollar exchange rate leads to a surge in stock prices due to strong exports, the reality is completely different: the Nikkei surged even as the yen-dollar exchange rate collapsed.

This is the proof that investing according to the Diamond Dollar Method works. If you look at [Figure 2], you would expect Japanese housing to rise in line with the rate of yen appreciation, but unfortunately, if you look at the graph of the housing index at the bottom, you can only see the sharp rise after 2010.

It is unfortunate that Japanese housing indexes prior to 2010 are not available, so we cannot compare the results, but according to the principle of the Diamond Dollar Investment Method, the Japanese housing index should have risen by the same percentage as the yen-dollar exchange rate fell.

And, indeed, it did. Looking at the spike in the housing index after the D-point, we can infer that it would have risen along with the Nikkei, albeit in the opposite direction, before the long term deflationary process.

From the three graphs above, you can see that real estate such as stocks and apartments are reflected in the yen's movements on a day-to-day basis, and they do not move exactly in an inverse relationship.

However, in the medium to long term, we can see that there is an inverse relationship with the yen-dollar exchange rate, meaning that when the exchange rate goes down, stocks go up and real estate goes up. Naturally, the reverse also happens.

Investors know from experience that stock prices reflect

changes in exchange rates on an almost daily basis. If you look down the vertical dotted line, you can see that it represents the change in the indicator in the same year and month.

Next, let's look at vertical lines ② and ③ at the same time.
Point B on the yen-dollar graph at vertical line ② is the short-term low point of the yen's rise. The line connecting point B and the vertical dotted line ② is the peak of the yen, so the Nikkei should be at or near the peak if we follow the Diamond Dollar Investment Method in [Figure 1].

Although the housing index for the same period is not available in the graph in [Figure 2], housing prices should have been at their peak. The housing index would have been at point B and the vertical dotted line ②. It would have been rising rapidly like the Nikkei, shown in the center.

Meanwhile, the yen.dollar price, which has made a short-term low, is rising sharply past the lowest point B, and the Nikkei index has risen sharply to reach the highest point in Japanese history C. The Nikkei was at 38,915 in December 1989, just before the crash.

In the vertical dotted lines ② and ③, the yen-dollar exchange rate and the Nikkei index are in direct proportion to each other. This is surprising. The diamond dollar investment method does not apply, i.e., the Nikkei surges as the yen rises. This is a clear and long-term result that defies common sense.

[Figure 2] shows that in the period before the second period, the yen-dollar exchange rate and the Nikkei were inversely correlated. Normally, when the yen rises, stock prices soar.

However, periods 2 and 3 in [Figure 2] are completely different from the period before period 2. The opposite phenomenon occurred.

As the dollar rose, stock prices rose in response. As the dollar rose, stock prices should have fallen, but instead, the relationship was inversely proportional.

Again, the housing index for the same period is not available and cannot be compared, but since the period after point D is a long term deflation, we can infer that the movement of the housing index in the short term deflation would have spiked in the period between ② and ③, just like the stock price.

In other words, in a long term deflation, the stock price and the country's exchange rate start to move in the same direction. It is important to remember this.

If we take a closer look, we can see that the vertical dotted lines ②and B indicate the start of the long term deflation. This is the period when the diamond dollar investing method starts to work in reverse. In other words, this is where the inverse diamond dollar investing method starts to work.

The stock index jumped 29% in the C-C' range, and the yen-dollar exchange rate jumped 30% in the B-B' range over the same one-year period. Contrary to common knowledge, the yen-dollar exchange rate is rising rapidly, and the Nikkei is also rising rapidly.

This is the phenomenon of long term deflation. Over the same one-year period, the housing index should have risen similarly. However, it is important to remember that there is always a six-month lag between the stock index and the housing index.

In this way, you can find the beginning of a long term deflation by looking at the direction of movement of the yen and stock indices on a daily basis.

If you find it, you will know that you need to change your investment method to the opposite of the method you have been investing in during short term deflation.

1) If you catch a long term deflation, you should never buy dollar deposits or invest abroad. This is because once a long term deflation begins, the price of the dollar will continue to decline, as shown in the top graphic in [Figure 2], after B'.

In the case of Japan, the price of the dollar in Japan has fallen by about 80% or more. If the dollar exchange rate, or the exchange rate of any country, falls by 80%, no one will survive. In short, if this happens, prices in any country drop by 80%, long term deflation is in full swing.

2) You should never invest in stocks or real estate. The reason for this can be seen in [Figure 2], which shows the Nikkei and housing indices.

Over the past 30 years, Japanese stocks and real estate, two of the top five assets for financial investment, have fallen by about 80-90%.

[Figure 2] shows a one-year period from December 1988 to December 1989 (B-B', a 30% spike) in Japan. During the same year or so, Korea's exchange rate barely changed from 687.40->681.40, which is surprising.

It is normal for the Korean and Japanese exchange rates to rise and fall almost every time in the same direction and by the same percentage.

The same phenomenon occurs in Korea as the dollar

falls in price during long term deflation. It is important to know whether the current deflation is short term or long term because it determines the performance of your investment in reverse, and you should invest and withdraw accordingly. The three are exactly inversely proportional.

This gives us a look into the future of gold's irrationally high price. Here's a look at the future of the gold price.
In a long term deflation, it is almost certain that there will be a period of low exchange rates for a significant period of time.

The dollar is just cash for Americans, so it's always a safe haven, but for everyone else, it's a monster asset that fluctuates wildly in price.

You can get rich by rotating your investments in the following order: stocks, apartments, dollars, deposits, and government bonds, depending on the movement of the dollar.

Short term forecasting of exchange rates is important, but you can't get rich if you don't anticipate the fluctuations in the price of your property in the medium to long term.

The most important thing is to recognize when we're looking at a transition to long term deflation. Unfortunately, there's no automatic way to do this, so you'll have to rely on day to day observation!

And the trick to recognizing a long term deflation in just one country is completely different from a long term deflation in the whole world at the same time.

Also, your investment approach should be completely different during a long deflation and a short deflation.

It's 180 degrees different. Needless to say, this is why it is essential to distinguish between long and short deflation.

Chapter 3)

The fall of riches: Your riches will fall like America's and Japan's.

In the U.S., stocks dropped 87% in a short period of time, and in Japan, apartments and stocks dropped up to 90%. Your wealth can be wiped out like this if you don't prepare!

Specific examples of wealth destruction due to long term deflation are the Great Depression in the 1930s in the US and Japan after 1990. When LongTerm Deflation(LTD) arrives, it will be so destructive that it will last for a long period of time, 10-30 years or more!

U.S. stocks crashed by 87.1% in two years and nine months, and Japanese stocks and apartments fell by up to 80-90% in a short period of time. When stocks and apartments crash due to long term deflation, they do not recover in a short period of time, as in the case of Korea's IMF crisis, the 2008 financial crisis, and the corona crisis.

The United States only escaped the Great Depression in 1950 after 22 years of steady decline. Japan only recovered after 32 years. No one can withstand such a long decline. That's why I say the dreaded LTD (Long Term Deflation) is coming.

The world is already in the midst of a long term deflation, with the $4.5 trillion of money released during the 2008 subprime crisis and the roughly $2.5 trillion of money released in the coronavirus now combined to support the global economy. Inflation is underway due to the temporary increase in money supply.

To the present, the economic community has labeled the U.S. as the Great Depression and Japan as the Lost 20 Years, but the author believes that both countries have been in a state of LTD.

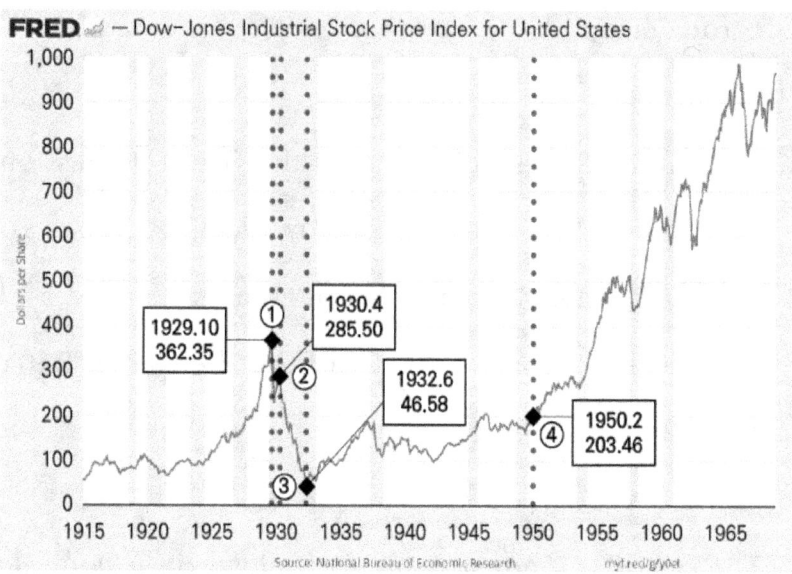

[Fig.3] Dow Jones long term graph(1914~1968)

[Figure 3] is a long-term graph of the Dow over a period of about 55 years, including the Great Depression. The vertical dotted lines ①②③ in [Figure 3] are the vertical dotted lines ①②③ in [Figure 6].

The vertical dotted line ④ in [Figure 3] shows that the United States, which experienced the Great Depression in 1929, did not escape the long term deflation until around 1950.

.The Dow broke through the 200-point resistance level in February 1950, a whopping 22 years after the Great Depression began. In other words, the U.S. was in deflation for 22 years after the Great Depression of 1929, well beyond the usual five-year timeframe for distinguishing between long and short term deflation.

The deflation experienced by the United States during this time was clearly a long term deflation, making the United States the first country in human history to experience a long term deflation. Japan emerged from a long term deflation a whopping 32 years later, in December 1988.

.

In fact, the next country destined to experience a LTD after the United States was Germany! Germany was experiencing a recession so severe that there was even talk of the country's demise before Japan.

As we all know, Germany was one of the 2 countries that signed the Plaza Agreement with the 6 Western countries on the same day as Japan.

However, Germany seems to have avoided the long term deflation by simply solving the working age population problem with the merger of East and West Germany on October 3, 1990.

South Korea is also in its ninth year of LTD, as its core working age population began shrinking in 2013, and China's working age population began shrinking in 2014.

The graph shows that the start date of the global LTD is 2016. However, it does not seem to be in full swing yet, and it is important to remember that the theories in this book are always applicable in any country.

Published in 1936 in the midst of the Great Depression in the United States, Keynes' General Theory was the first proper economic theory of its kind, primarily analyzing the ills of the capitalist economy of the 1930s: unemployment and depression.

Keynesian economics is also known as the theory of effective demand, and today's recession is the result of a lack of effective demand due to a declining population, excessive debt, etc. Effective demand is purchasing power.

Like the popular term "working age population," it is better to interpret it as a shortage of consumers rather than a production-oriented perspective. If you turn the working age population upside down, it becomes the consumption age population.

Let's start with two graphs!
[Figure 4] does not show the change in land prices in Japan up to the present day, which is what we need, and is only available up to 2007. This graph shows 1974 at 100.

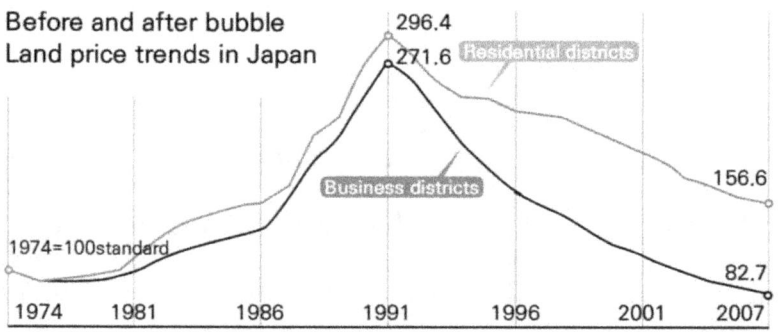

[Fig.4] Land prices in Japan before and after the 1990 bubble burst (Source: Ministry of Land, Infrastructure, Transport and Tourism)

We can see that commercial land prices in 2007 are about 17.3% lower than they were in 1974, or 45 years ago, and 69.6% lower than they were at the peak in 1991.

Residential land, on the other hand, is 56.6% higher than it was 34 years ago in 1974. However, in 2007, it is still 47.1% below its 1991 peak price.

The Tokyo and Chiba New Town Apartment Price Index, or Housing Index, in [Figure 5] is a long-term price graph of condominiums (equivalent to apartments in Korea) in Tokyo and Chiba New Town from 1993 to 2018.

It can be seen that housing prices (land + building) have increased by about 12.5% as of 2018 compared to 2010.

[Figure 4] and [Figure 5] are transcribed directly from the author's book, Tears of the Japanese, as they are important to the logical development. I will give full credit later when the source is known.

The housing indices for Chiba New Town and Tokyo are plotted against a price index of 100 in June 1993. The Japanese real estate crash started on April 1, 1990. 33 years after the bubble burst this year in Japan.

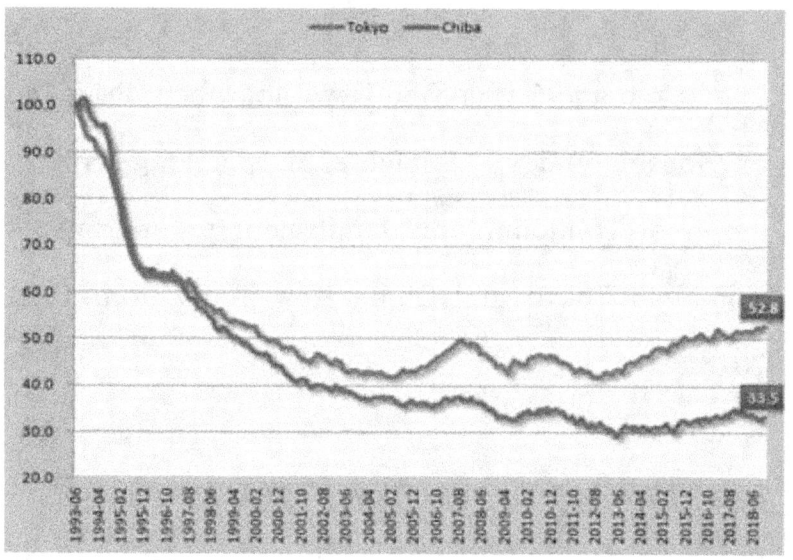

[Fig.5] Apts price index for Tokyo and Chiba New Town. 1993=100 (Source: Japan Real Estate Research Institute)

In fact, when a bubble bursts, real estate and stocks usually experience a significant drop in price for about three to five years.

If we look at the Nikkei, the center figure in [Figure 2], we can see that it was January 1990 38,915

14,517 in June 1995

and 7,568 in February 2009.

In June 1995, the index was about 62.7% of its peak,

In February 2009, the index plunged 80.5% from its 1990 peak.

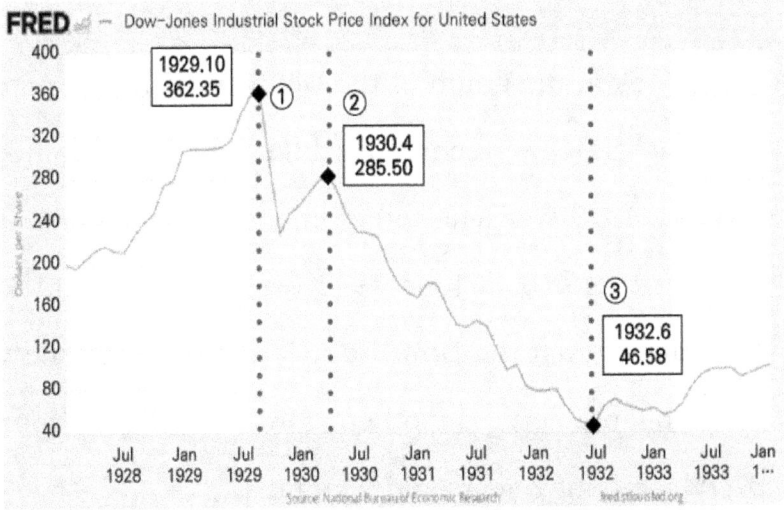

[Fig.6] Graph of the Dow Jones Index

[Figure 3] is a graph of the Dow Jones during the Great

Depression of 1929. You can see that the Dow Jones Index went from 285.50 points in April 1930 to 46.58 points in June 1932, a drop of 83.7% in just two years and three months.

In the 1920s, land speculation reached its peak in the U.S. state of Florida, where a piece of land in Miami Beach, which cost $800 in 1921, was worth $150,000 in 1924.

If you look at the graph of the Dow at that time, you can see that the Dow recorded a high of 362.35 points in October 1929 (vertical dotted line ①), and compared to the low of 46.58 in June 1932 (vertical dotted line ③), you can see that the Dow dropped dramatically and was at a collapse level. In other words, the Dow dropped 87.1% in about 2 years and 9 months.

In this case, if you had invested those funds in cash and

cash equivalents, such as government bonds, deposits, or home equity, you could have earned a thrilling return while other people's wealth, or wealth, was being destroyed by 87.1% in one fell swoop.

The difference in wealth would be maximized by an 87.1% surge in relative value, a modest increase in absolute value due to dividends, and a surge in the price of cash and cash equivalents as interest rates fall.

In other words, the difference between the returns of investors who are prepared for a long period of deflation and the average investor would be unimaginable.

Long term deflation is the opportunity for readers of my book to make the great transformation from laborer to capitalist, from poor to get rich. According to the author's proven diamond-shaped dollar investing method, stocks and real estate always change at roughly the same rate.

Therefore, if you don't react to a LTD, but simply hold on to your wealth during a long term deflation, as you did during the past 70 years of inflation, your wealth will shrink by 80-90% on average.

No one can survive an 80-90% collapse in property prices like in the US or Japan. Modern people use bank loans or credit, so almost everyone's equity is 50% or less.

When the market crashes like this, your equity is already gone and you're left with bank debt. You'll be a complete tin foil hat investor.

In addition, Korea, China, and Japan use a system of subordination that allows them to seize a borrower's other assets until the debt is repaid, so borrowers are stuck until the debt is paid.

Simple rich people who have never studied finance, who got rich through inheritance or just holding real estate for the long term, are much more likely to be unaware of this.

They have successfully made their fortune by simply holding onto it for the long term, using leverage.

everyone should have already exchanged all their possessions for cash and cash equivalents, because if you don't prepare for a LTD, you are destined for poverty.

These facts have been researched, proven, and demonstrated by the author for the first time. You can't get them from any other book, from anyone. In conclusion, investors need to know and be prepared for the unseen future as well as the past.

During the 22 years of the US Great Depression in 1929, the stocks of the wealthy declined by up to 87.1%. It wasn't until 1950 that they broke through the index resistance.

We don't know much about house prices at the time, but they must have crashed in proportion to stocks, because the Diamond Dollar method of investing hasn't changed since then.

On the other hand, Japan entered a LTD around December 1988, and after a year of simultaneous appreciation of the dollar, stocks, and apartments by about 30%, Japanese stocks crashed by about 80-90% over the next 30 years from January 4, 1990, and real estate such as apartments crashed by about 80% over the next 30 years from April 1, 1990.

Over the next 32 years, 80-90% of Japanese who held onto their stocks and real estate must have lost money.

A crash of this proportion is unstoppable!
If the price does not recover for such a long period of time, it will fall forever!

These facts of the past U.S. history should make everyone thoroughly prepare for the upcoming Long-Term Deflation!
So, let's take a look at what causes a long deflation, how to recognize the signs, how to invest successfully during a long deflation, and more.

Chapter 4)

Causes of Long Term Deflation (1)Dollar Weakness

Specific causes of long term deflation include a weak dollar, declining population, and overindebtedness. The discovery of robots and superconductors are other causes. Of these, a weaker dollar is the most powerful and largest cause. Dollar weakness is indiscriminate, immediate, and powerful.

Let's take a quick look at the most powerful cause of Japan's long term deflation: the change in the yen-dollar exchange rate [Figure 7].

In January 1971, it took 357.72 yen to buy a dollar.
In January 2012, you could buy a dollar for only 76.34 yen. In September 2021, you could buy a dollar for

110.61 yen.

In September 2023, I had to pay 146.20 yen to buy a dollar. Compared to January 2012, the Japanese domestic dollar has fallen 78.7% in 42 years.

Compared to September 2021, the price of the domestic dollar is still 31% lower than it was in January 1971, 51 years ago.

.

By 2012,

the dollar crashed.

apartments crashed.

stocks crashed.

interest rates and mortgage rates collapsed.

These are just a few of the things that go up in a LTD.

So if you invest in any country that is already in long term deflation, there will be nowhere left to invest your money.past. Like Japan, there's nothing left to invest in.

It's all because of long term deflation.

Long term deflation has come to the world, and it will destroy everything for 5~30 years!
This is the difference between long term deflation and short term deflation, i.e. a normal recession. As the Korean won strengthens, prices in Korea are bound to go down. Therefore, the continuous decline of the dollar is the most powerful cause of deflation.

A 3% drop in the price of the dollar reduces the price of all imports by 3%, so you have an incentive to cut your salary by 3% because things are cheaper. A decline in the price of the dollar becomes a deflation rate that applies indiscriminately to prices.

Conversely, an increase in the price of the dollar, or an appreciation of the exchange rate, raises the price of imports and raises the price of exports, giving the exporting country or company an excess gain on the exchange rate. Therefore, countries around the world tend to favor high exchange rate policies.

As a result, the U.S. sometimes designates countries with intentionally high exchange rates as currency manipulators, while other times they are more loosely monitored. All countries have economic policies that serve their own purposes, but almost all have high exchange rates.

Depending on the scholar, Barry Eichengreen, a professor at UC Berkeley, predicts that the "king dollar" is here to stay. The US national debt is high, but not insurmountable, and there is no new currency that will replace it, he argues. In other words, the dollar is still the absolute safe haven.

For the most part, I agree with him, but he doesn't seem

to realize that in a long term deflation, any country will have a weak domestic dollar. He is an American living in the United States, so he has never experienced the power of the dollar.

I explain Japan's "lost 32 years" as an example. We can start by looking at the evolution of the yen-dollar exchange rate within Japan.

The yen-dollar exchange rate before and after the Plaza Accord on September 22, 1985, was 79% at its peak.

The price of the dollar crashed by up to 79%. Of course, at that time, only Japanese domestic dollar prices fell, but since the current long term deflation has hit everywhere except Japan, it means that domestic dollar prices fell all over the world except Japan.

Take a look at [Figure 5], a graph of the yen-dollar

exchange rate over 50 years. Consistent with the theory of the Diamond Dollar Investment Method described earlier, domestic Japanese assets have been crashing and burning for more than 30 years.

The yen-dollar exchange rate has plummeted by as much as 79%, and as the yen-dollar exchange rate falls, the price of all imported goods falls proportionally by 79%. As a result, prices in Japan continue to fall by the same amount as the yen-dollar exchange rate.

Japanese stocks plunged 80% in response. Japan's longest period of deflation, which began in December 1989, lasted 32 years.

When prices rise, companies make more money, governments collect more taxes, and households get more money. Increased income, whether in real or nominal terms, creates a monetary illusion that motivates economic entities to engage in economic activity.

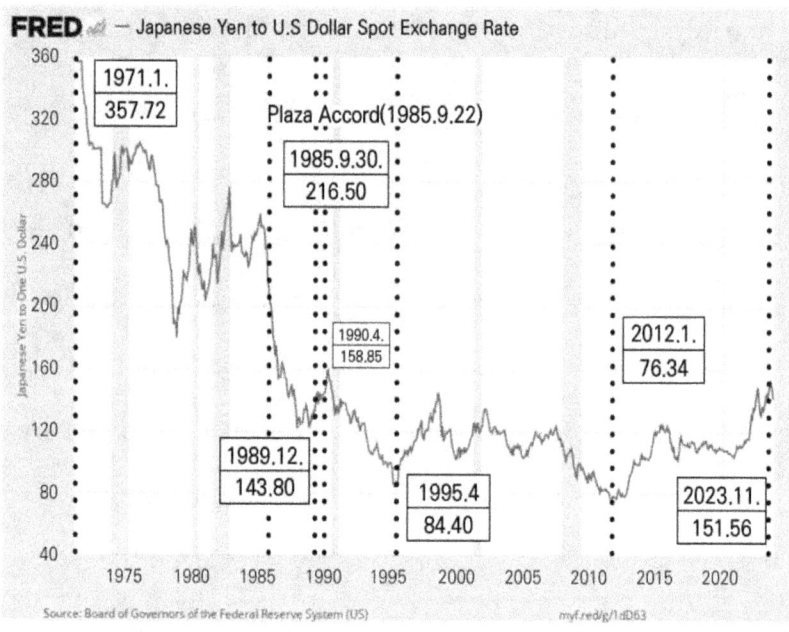

[Fig.7] Yen to Dollar Exchange Rate Graph

However, when everything goes down for more than 30 years, society loses its vitality and becomes less motivated to work. In [Figure 7], in January 1971, the yen to dollar exchange rate was 357.72 yen.

Forty-two years later, in January 2012, the yen.dollar

exchange rate was 76.34 yen. From 1971 to 2012, the yen jumped by a whopping 78.7%. There were some ups and downs along the way, but that's more than 32 years of crashing dollar prices in Japan.

So the economy loses momentum, and there's nowhere to invest. Eventually, interest rates on deposits and loans plummeted to 0%. With the long term deflation, nothing was going up. There was nothing to invest in among Japan's domestic assets.

This is because of the long term deflation caused by the falling exchange rate. The continuous decline in the yen-dollar exchange rate is due to the Plaza Accord, but it is also due to the accumulation of excessive trade surpluses year after year. The supply of dollars in Japan has always been excessive and excessive.

Therefore, financial firms began to solicit overseas

investments. Ordinary investors in Japan invested in overseas stocks and dividend stocks at the recommendation of securities professionals, financial companies, or the government. Japan became the world's number one creditor of overseas financial assets, with $3.5 trillion, about two years of GDP.

The result of the investment was a slight increase in local asset prices, but if the investments are returned to Japan, rather than leaving money behind, the yen's continued strength (dollar weakness) caused foreign investors to lose a lot of money due to exchange losses. Eventually, overseas investment funds became ghost dollars that could not be brought back into Japan.

In terms of results alone, this means that Japanese people have run out of places to invest since January 1971, 42 years ago, both domestically and overseas. All investment sources have evaporated. It's really a huge thing.

So naturally, the Japanese economy lost its vitality and the short term deflation became stuck in the long term deflation. Conventional measures against short term deflation have been ineffective.

None of the economic policies worked, and the Japanese economy became less and less energized as the years went by. The problem is the long term deflation that is now upon the world.

Korea and the rest of the world will end up like Japan in 1989, with nowhere to invest after a 30-50% surge in stocks and apartments, reflecting a surge in the price of the local currency and a sharp drop in the NAV(Net Asset Value.NAV) of the US dollar.

The conclusion of the leading stock theory, which was

established by a famous Korean securities company after 32 years of intensive analysis of Korean leading stocks, is that "leading stocks usually rise 4-20 times in 3-4 years, and when the leading stocks are bubble breaking, they fall by 80-90%. The author believes that this theory is true in any country and any era.

In the case of Korea, the great bull market that started in May 2017 is expected to peak in June 2021. The peak for apartments will be in December 2021. As expected, this is what happened. It is surprising that the year and month were exactly the same.

This last surge is due to the decline in the price of the dollar, the international dollar price, so even if you completely block bank loans, it will surge, so the government's bank loan regulation measures are useless. We have experienced this before. This is because it is a reflection of the Net Asset Value (NAV) due to the surge in the Korean won-dollar exchange rate.

After this final rise, Korea, like Japan, will have nothing to invest in. Not only Korea, but the entire world will be in the same situation as long term deflation will soon be in full swing, except for Japan.

As soon as the short-lived inflation caused by the subprime crisis in 2008 and the coronavirus in 2020 ends, the world will fall into the vortex of long term deflation. Of the various causes of long term deflation, the most powerful is the indiscriminate depreciation of exchange rates across all prices.

In a long term deflation like Japan's, no one can do anything right economic policy. The U.S. is also in a long term deflation, so it is not enough to respond to it by printing money infinitely like Japan's Abenomics policy, but the U.S. is currently engaged in a reshoring policy that reduces the supply of dollars around the world. A strong dollar policy and a weak dollar are going hand in hand.

Meanwhile, these ghostly Japanese investments, which haunt international financial markets, seek to return home whenever the global economy is in crisis.

This is the curse of the yen. If any country's investments are going abroad with vague expectations, these funds are destined to turn into the "curse of the yen," "curse of the won," "curse of the yuan," and so on.

In other words, if the Korean investments go abroad, they will not be able to bring them back to Korea due to the surge in the exchange rate of the won. Just like now, Japanese people have completely run out of places to invest since 30 years ago.

The changes in the yen-dollar exchange rate, the Nikkei index, and the housing index after the BC'② line in [Figure 2] show that Japan's yen-dollar exchange rate and stocks and real estate have collapsed.

As you can see, the losses have been piling up for more than 30 years as you invest in stocks, real estate, small buildings, bank deposits, dollar deposits, gold, etc. There is nowhere to invest. This is the phenomenon of long term deflation.

Long-term deflation destroys the economy for a long period of time like 5~ 30 years, so I mentioned earlier that the Japanese didn't want to buy a house to live in, let alone a house to rent. The Japanese were smart in this regard.

Japanese investments already abroad amount to $3.5 trillion, i.e. two years of GDP. While the exchange rate at the time of investment abroad varies from a high of 360 yen to a low of 75 yen, on average, the loss in foreign currency conversion alone is more than 50 to 80 percent of the investment when it returns to Japan.

The "Curse of the Safe Currency" The term "curse of the yen", first proposed by Professor Barry Eichengreen of the University of California, Berkeley, refers to the phenomenon that the demand for the yen, which is treated as a safe currency internationally, increases whenever a financial crisis occurs. As a result, the yen actually becomes stronger in the event of a financial crisis.

The curse of the yen refers to a phenomenon in which the value of the dollar or euro crashes due to a financial crisis, and the price of the yen should also fall at the same time, but instead, the yen increases slightly or decreases only slightly compared to the dollar or euro.

The curse of the safe-haven currency comes from the case of the Japanese yen, whose value does not reflect the economic situation. More recently, during the 2008 financial crisis, when the euro crashed and the pound plunged following Brexit, the yen and yen-denominated government bonds actually rose.

In other words, the yen was an alternative investment destination and exit for investors. After 2008, the yen jumped to a whopping 75 yen. This is what happened for 30 lost years, but now, thanks to Abenomics, Japan is out of long term deflation. Abenomics is all about devaluing the yen.

The yen does not weaken as expected during a global economic crisis, but rather strengthens slightly, as people wait for the foreign exchange losses to decrease even a little and try to bring a lot of money into Japan at once.

Some people say that the reason for the curse of the yen is that it is a safe haven asset, but this is not the whole story, because the yen is not the only safe haven asset, the dollar and the pound are also safe haven assets. The price of the dollar in Japan has fallen from 360 yen to 75 yen over time and is now over 150 yen.

Since 1989, Japan has seen a 30% surge in the yen-dollar exchange rate in about a year and a 29% surge in the Nikkei index over the same period. This phenomenon is impossible to explain. It cannot be explained by common sense.

[Figure 2] illustrates this fact.

In the one-year period from December 1988 to December 1989, the Nikkei surged 29%. This is the C'-C interval. In the one year and four months from December 1988 to April 1990, the yen-dollar exchange rate jumped 30%. This is B-B'. When the yen-dollar exchange rate rises, the Nikkei should drop. Instead, both the exchange rate and stock prices rose dramatically.

This has nothing to do with the Plaza Accord. The Plaza Accord was signed on September 22, 1985. The IMF in Korea started on December 3, 1997. The Seoul Olympics were held in September 1988, which is not at all possible according to common sense.

However, it is also common knowledge that it would not be related to the Seoul Olympics, i.e., there was no event. The author has been cautiously watching for this to happen in Korea.

But now that we're past that, the world is expecting the Great Depression, or Long Term Deflation, to begin in earnest after a brief period of inflation.

In Japan, long term deflation has been in full swing since then, and Japanese stocks and real estate have plummeted by about 80-90%.

The author believes that Korea is in a long term deflationary situation like Japan in the past, which is why stocks and real estate have plummeted so much.

The government and some academics have been saying that we are different from Japan, which is to say that there is no real estate price crash in Korea, and there is no deflation.

However, neither Korea nor the world is safe from asset market crashes like Japan. A temporary boom in the asset market followed by a subsequent crash starts with the bursting of a bubble.

Although Korea's currency is not an international currency, it may be subject to the curse of the won in the future, similar to Japan's yen phenomenon, which occurs in times of crisis. In other words, the 'curse of the won' may appear.

Considering Korea's strong economy based on the world's No. 1 and 2 manufacturing competitiveness, huge foreign exchange reserves, and unlimited currency swap agreements with major economies such as Canada and Switzerland, the Korean won is expected to be a currency with little fluctuation in the future, and will likely strengthen in times of crisis.

This is an opportunity for salarymen and poor people to go from laborers to capitalists. It is a stroke of genius to sell an asset that has fallen by 90% and sell an asset that has risen by 90% and make a fortune 10 times over.

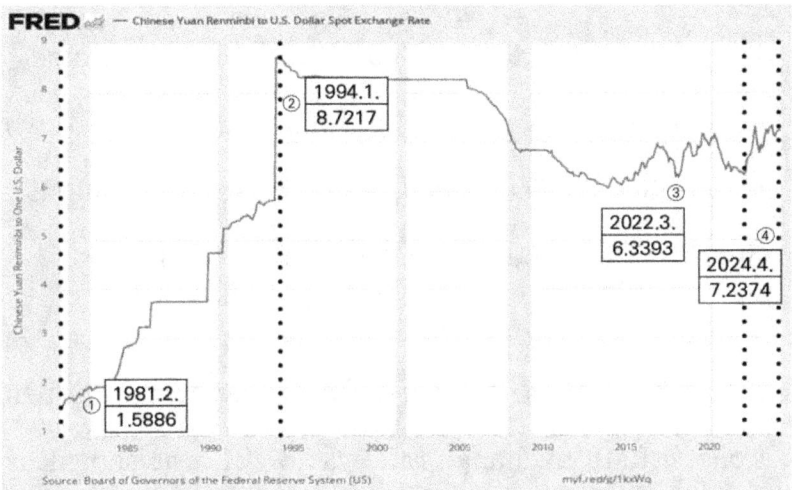

[Fig.8] Yuan.Dollar Graph

Developing countries can most easily make their products more competitive abroad by adjusting their exchange rates. In other words, the simplest way to gain international price competitiveness is to raise the exchange rate.

China first entered the global market and easily gained competitiveness thanks to the constant appreciation of the yuan, as shown in [Figure 8].

In other words, as shown in vertical dotted line ① in [Figure 8], China has continuously appreciated the exchange rate between the dollar and the RMB, which was 1.5886 on February 1, 1981, close to the initial year of reform and opening up (December 1978).

In February 1994, 14 years after the reform and opening up, the RMB exchange rate was 8.7217, as shown in ②. That's a whopping 549.0% devaluation of the RMB.

Since then, the yuan has been strengthening. At the end of April 2024, it was 7.2374 yuan per dollar. This is a 20.5% appreciation from the peak price, and China appears to be in the midst of a long term deflation.

It is simply a 20.5% drop in the price of all goods. Think of the lost 30 years of Japan and make a judgment.

Since joining the WTO in 2001, China has successfully entered the global market with the cheap labor of its 1.4 billion people and competitive prices for its products.

This has helped the world enjoy nearly 40 years of inflation-free boom. Thus, China became a G2 economy in about 40 years after its reform and opening up in 1978.

When Korea first entered the international market, it also aimed to increase exports by securing international price competitiveness through a high exchange rate policy. However, this step is not easy to apply after a certain period of time because importing countries are accumulating deficits.

Winning the global market on price alone is neither permanent nor indefinite. The cost of labor, land, etc. will skyrocket.

As China has replaced our market with cheap products and an appreciating yuan, some of the three factors of production, namely 3M (materials, man, and money), must be at an absolute advantage to secure price competitiveness in the international market.

When price competitiveness starts to decline, it is necessary to strengthen quality competitiveness, which is competing with quality. The same product, but the price-quality ratio must be upgraded to the next level to be competitive in the international market.

IIn today's world, a product sells when the price-performance ratio is right. If the quality is excellent, the price can be passed on even when the exchange rate depreciates.

Continuous capital outflows. If the exchange rate continues to decline, dollar-denominated assets increase, which naturally creates a temptation for capital outflows.

If we take Japan as an example, the price of the dollar in Japan is constantly falling, so when Japanese people look at U.S. assets, it's as if the asset price has collapsed, but from an American perspective, the price of U.S. assets remains the same. That is, it hasn't moved at all. It's not going up, it's not going down.

However, the decline in the dollar's price pushes up the valuation of Japanese assets, which tempts capital outflows from Japan. In turn, Japan's GDP favors outflows, which in turn causes a decline in domestic consumption, which in turn increases the temptation for dollar outflows, creating a vicious cycle.

The bottom line is that excessive current account surpluses, or exports, are a detriment to the yen.
Japanese people look for the dollar's lowest point when investing abroad, and if they don't get it, they end up losing money.

If the price of the dollar continues to fall even after that, they can't even bring home the money they spent abroad. The amount of overseas investment just keeps growing and accumulating.

It also means that Japanese money invested abroad after 32 years is about to get a complete windfall because Abenomics was successful.

Abenomics was all about making Japan more

competitive internationally by freeing up money to depreciate the yen.

If the low yen is brought about by Abenomics and U.S. asset prices rise, the return on investment + exchange rate gains for Japanese investors abroad will be enormous.

For this to happen, Japan's national power and competitiveness must be weakened and the yen must weaken. Intentional monetization would have the same effect.

In the end, the huge trade surplus is one of the most powerful reasons why Japan is in trouble. If Japan wants to survive, it needs to reduce its trade surplus.

Japan has long term deflation, which means that even if you keep your assets in the country, they will fall in price every year. If you take them out of the country instead, they don't fall as much.

However, the money that goes out of the country is brought back into the country with a stronger yen, resulting in exchange losses. This is the Japanese dilemma. It can also be a dilemma for South Koreans and Chinese.

The Plaza Accords of September 22, 1985, saw about a twofold strengthening of the yen. Real estate and stocks in Japan skyrocket according to the understanding of the Diamond Dollar Investment Method [Figure 1].

In the case of Japan, it actually increased by about 300% between 1986 and 1989. This is the situation before the vertical dotted line BC'② in [Figure 2].

Look at the surge in the Nikkei index during this period. The peak price was almost tripled as the market searched for an equilibrium point.

But after the great collapse of Japan in 1990, it is now down 80-90% due to long term deflation.

This is due to the collapse of the dollar, population issues, and debt issues, but the biggest reason is the collapse of the yen to the dollar. Now it's time to look at the population issue.

Chapter 5)

Is South Korea's foreign exchange reserve adequate for a so-called dollar ATM country?

Think of forex, i.e the dollar, as a Paleolithic shell currency. Imagine you want to buy a computer, a cell phone, or anything else, and the other person only recognizes and accepts shells as currency.

In this case, everyone would have to have shells, and the more shells you have, the more foreign goods you can buy. Imagine that people in the country use a different currency to trade with each other.

They needed to pay their debts, and they temporarily didn't have this shell currency. This was mainly due to short-term foreign currency debt borrowed from other countries.

The consequences of the bite, bite, bite of the global economy getting stuck in the backward Asian countries were beginning to affect Korea.

There are two ways to obtain the dollar: by leaving money in and out of the country and filling the national treasury, and by borrowing foreign currency from banks, companies, and governments. Overseas, you can't buy dollars with Korean money. They don't recognize the Korean won as a currency.

Dollars can only flow into Korea if foreigners buy foreign currency-backed government bonds issued by Korea, such as through the difference between imports and exports or foreign currency borrowing. Otherwise, foreigners can only spend dollars through domestic travel.

Dollars also flow into Korea when foreigners establish or co-invest in companies in Korea, or when they bring in dollars to buy stocks or real estate.

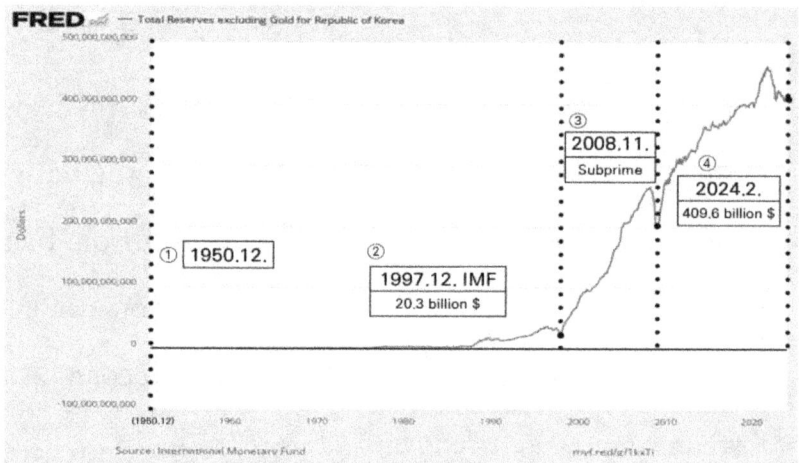

[Fig.9] South Korea's foreign exchange reserves excluding gold, (1950.12~2024.2)

[Figure 18] shows South Korea's foreign exchange reserves, excluding gold. As of January 2023, it was $407 billion. When companies import and export dollars, the difference is either deposited in a company's foreign currency account or exchanged directly into KRW.

In order to block the adverse effects of rapid fluctuations in the exchange rate, the government intervenes in the foreign exchange market to stabilize the foreign exchange market through the purchase and sale of foreign exchange, and the fund created by the government is called the 'Foreign Exchange Equilibrium Fund'.

The Foreign Exchange Equilibrium Fund can be used in cases deemed necessary by the government, such as emergencies that occur when importing foreign exchange.

Whether businesses or individuals hold dollars in foreign currency deposits or exchange them, all dollars entering the country are held by the government.

Commercial banks are required to hold only a small

amount of foreign currency in reserve for payments and entrust the entire amount to the Bank of Korea (the government). This is the foreign exchange reserve, and eventually all foreign currency is centralized by the government.

If the entire amount is issued as a foreign exchange balancing fund bond, the interest will also be paid from the national treasury, so only a certain amount will be issued according to the amount of currency in the market at the time.

The issuance of foreign exchange balancing fund bonds is used to control the amount of currency in the market, but it can also adjust the exchange rate. Central banks can also buy or sell dollars directly on the foreign exchange market to adjust the exchange rate.

It's also worth noting that these are the only two ways a

country can adjust its exchange rate. However, the difference between these inflows and outflows is a fraction of GDP, or the amount of money a country earns in a year, and collecting it in foreign equilibrium fund bonds is equivalent to reducing the welfare of the population.

In other words, it's forced savings. In any case, all the dollars in the country are centrally managed by the BOK on behalf of the government. The dollar is also subject to the laws of supply and demand, so it makes sense that a large foreign exchange reserve would reduce short-term price fluctuations.

Currently, the market capitalization of Korean stocks held by foreigners is less than 600 trillion won, but when converted to dollars, it is about 500 billion dollars. As of January 2023, we have $424 billion, so it won't happen in any case, but if foreigners sell all their stocks and leave Korea, we will immediately be in an IMF situation.

Meanwhile, foreigners are investing huge amounts of dollars not only in Korean stocks but also in government bonds and real estate.

Korea is a so-called "dollar ATM country". Due to its high dependence on trade, Korea is easily exposed to financial and foreign exchange crises, and monthly trade volume by industry is used as an indicator for global economic forecasts.

It is also known as a "dollar ATM country" because it is possible to withdraw and deposit the required amount of dollars at any time like an automatic teller machine. This means that it is a country where foreign exchange is free to flow in and out.

However, even if there is a financial crisis or economic

crisis in a third country other than Korea, Korea often withdraws dollar funds first, so I am not sure whether the nickname "dollar ATM country" is good or bad.

The U.S. government also wants a weaker dollar to reduce its trade deficit. It's true that the US wants a weak dollar. This means that the won is likely to stay strong. A weaker dollar and a stronger won are likely to be the main topics of conversation for quite some time to come.

South Korea is unlikely to be able to increase its foreign exchange reserves for the foreseeable future as the U.S. looks to designate it a currency manipulator. Japan's foreign exchange reserves were $1.2 trillion as of March 2023, while China's were around $3.19 trillion. Even the U.S. has about $36.6 billion in foreign exchange (USD) in reserves.

Foreigners hold about 600 trillion won in Korean stocks alone, and there is also a huge amount of money in government bonds and real estate purchases.

Therefore, we are always worried about the adequacy of our current foreign exchange reserves, but there are many ways to evaluate the adequacy of foreign exchange reserves, usually based on GDP or monthly trade transactions.

According to the IMF and the Bank for International Settlements (BIS), adequate foreign exchange reserves are estimated to be between $280 billion and $440 billion, taking into account domestic imports, currency volume, and foreign securities investments.

As of 2022, South Korea's adequate foreign exchange reserves ratio was 97%, the lowest since 2000. The IMF considers adequate foreign exchange reserves to be 100-

150% of the sum of 5% of annual exports, 5% of money in circulation (M2), 30% of liquid foreign debt, and 15% of the balance of foreign securities and other investments.

Taken together, we're still hungry. In 2020, we were at 114% of our reserves. It's been falling for three years now, first at 99% in 2020 and then at a steady decline.

The reason for this is that short-term foreign debt has been growing faster than foreign exchange reserves. It is also important to note that the interest rate differential between Korea and the US has increased.

More is better, but it's hard to say exactly how much is too much, and the more you pile on, the less welfare you create.Since March 2022, the Fed has raised the U.S. benchmark interest rate by about 2,200%, from 0.25% to 5.5%, including four consecutive big steps.

As a result, the valuation of U.S. Treasuries held by central banks as foreign exchange reserves has plummeted. Since U.S. Treasuries are supposed to be valued at market price when determining foreign exchange reserves, Korea's foreign exchange reserves must have decreased significantly.

In addition, I believe that there will be several more interest rate hikes in the future and that they will last for a long time.

Therefore, we believe that all central banks around the world will revaluate their holdings of U.S. Treasuries as foreign exchange reserves, which will be reflected on their balance sheets, reducing their reserves.

After the 2008 financial crisis, another form of foreign exchange reserves, SWAP, was introduced between countries.

It's like a country's negative bank account in another country with which it has an agreement. These are funds that can only be accessed when needed.

Any country, including the U.S., can be caught in a financial pinch by temporarily running out of dollar cash, as happened to South Korea in the IMF crisis.

All it takes is for the world to accumulate foreign exchange reserves and the dollar becomes illiquid, so the U.S. will moderately increase its printing of dollars to prevent unnecessary appreciation.

The euro, yen, and yuan can also be used for foreign payments, but no country likes them. Recently, China, Russia, Saudi Arabia, Brazil, and a few other countries joined China's CHIPS in against SWIFT in the US, but the amount of usage is as good as nothing compared to the dollar.

In addition, countries that trade a lot can trade without using the dollar if they exchange trade funds in the other country's currency.

To reduce the use of the dollar, they can also reduce the amount of foreign exchange reserves in dollars, which is why there are currency SWAPs between China, Korea, Japan, and the United States.

The currency SWAP with Canada, signed in May 2017, is indefinite and unlimited. This year, we also entered into a currency SWAP agreement with Switzerland, which indirectly includes us in the foreign exchange safety net of a major currency.

So far, South Korea's indirect foreign currency holdings through SWAP agreements have totaled about $130 billion, or 33% of its existing foreign exchange reserves.

However, the dollar issuers, the world's leading reserve currency, have no reason to like SWAP agreements. While this would reduce the use of the dollar, it would also prevent them from enjoying the signorage effect. That's why I don't think a direct SWAP between Korea and the US is possible.

Also, since the majority of our foreign exchange reserves are in dollars, we need to use them to grow our money. This can be done with gold, U.S. bonds, or a certain amount of liquidity, which is why we keep a significant amount in dollar cash.

The Bank of Korea has signed an agreement with the U.S. Federal Reserve to utilize the repo system up to a limit of $60 billion in 2021.

The repo system is a system in which the U.S. Federal Reserve provides U.S. dollar-denominated funds to foreign central banks by purchasing U.S. Treasury bonds held by foreign central banks with the condition of repurchase.

Until now, the proof that South Korea's foreign exchange reserves are still insufficient has been that the price of the dollar always surges in South Korea during a crisis, but this may change.

The top four safe-haven assets are gold, the dollar, the Swiss franc, and the yen. Safe-haven assets are favored by investors in times of economic instability.

Due to the high demand, the price of safe-haven assets often goes up during a crisis. This is the case with the yen. The same goes for the US dollar. This is the dollar smiley phenomenon.

In a crisis, Japanese funds invested abroad and people from other countries buy yen. However, this is not always the case, as shown by the sharp drop in the value of the Japanese yen and the drop in the Nikkei index when Japan faced the IMF in 1998.

Chapter 6)

High vs. low US dollar exchange rate policies

The exchange rate of the dollar affects international payments of countries around the world, which in turn affects their economies. Therefore, countries prefer to maintain a high dollar exchange rate, knowing that it is advantageous to increase their exchange rate.

If we analyze Japan, long term deflation means a persistent weakness of the dollar, and as much as we all fear inflation, the persistent weakness of the dollar price due to long term deflation is actually more frightening. Just look at Japan's lost 30 years.

Currency exchange rates are complicated and overwhelming, and most people would prefer to live without worrying about them. However, everyone is already 100% exposed to the dollar exchange rate and cannot avoid it in their daily lives.

If the USD goes up in your country, the price of your favorite cup of coffee goes up, and if you go on vacation to a neighboring country, you'll notice that the cost of your trip goes up when you convert your currency.

What's more, even if you're a small business owner, an increase in the price of the USD can mean more foreign customers. Foreigners can get more Korean money for the same dollar.

So it's hard to live without paying attention to the US dollar exchange rate. They play a crucial role in determining the price of everything.

In normal times, it's a small change, but when the exchange rate spikes due to a foreign exchange crisis or economic crisis, you should know that it can cut your property in half. You don't want to think about it, but you should always be aware that the price of your property will change regardless of your will and regardless of domestic prices.

Governments are always trying to keep the dollar exchange rate stable because it affects people's daily lives. Except when it's unavoidable, they usually have it under control. That's why the dollar exchange rate often appears as a major policy objective.

12) US dollar high exchange rate policy

Every politician wants inflation to be around 2% per year. They expand the economy enough to cause 2% inflation every year. They want a moderate inflation of 2% per year, so that people will work hard because of the Monetary Illusion(a phenomenon in which people think that their income has simply increased in value, when in fact it has not).

They want people to be content and not pay attention to politics. In other words, moderate inflation is the best shortcut to long-term power, and the easiest policy for a politician or government to achieve long-term power is to keep the U.S. dollar high. Then they hope to be rewarded in the next election.

The easiest economic policy for politicians and governments to achieve this goal is to keep the U.S. dollar high. They expect the exchange rate to rise modestly each year, and they focus all their resources on maintaining the high exchange rate. A high US dollar exchange rate causes inflation because it indiscriminately raises the price of imports.

A high or modestly high exchange rate makes large

corporations fatter while the small businesses and salaried workers who supply them lose money in real terms.

The difference is then transferred to the exporters, which is why it's sometimes called an exchange rate tax.
It's also an inflationary tax because it brings inflation with it, which means it's really just a tax.

Here's how it works: when a large company receives an export order, it will order parts to be delivered to an small company.

The small business has to import the raw materials for the parts or manufacture them themselves.
In other words, about 6 months later, the parts are delivered to the exporting conglomerate, and the conglomerate assembles them into a finished product, which is then exported.

After the large company exports, the export payment is received 2-3 months later, and the small business usually doesn't get paid for the goods until a year after delivery.

In the meantime, the exchange rate continues to gradually rise, and the large company gets a free exchange rate when it exchanges the export payment for the local currency.
For large companies, this exchange rate gain alone can be enough to pay their employees' salaries.

In the meantime, if the price of goods rises and becomes inflationary, the selling price of domestic goods will also have to be raised, giving exporters a double benefit of free money.

On the other hand, small and medium-sized enterprises that need to supply large companies are faced with a huge price increase in raw materials due to the exchange rate.

The small business is made worse because large corporations don't pay them 100% of the cost of imported raw materials.

This is the same as an exchange rate tax, an inflation tax.

If the exchange rate increases by 10% (let's say 100 won), how much does a large company earn?

A study once showed that about 67% of the export value, i.e. 67 won, would increase in big companies' profits.

2) US dollar low exchange rate policy

As deflation progresses and the US dollar depreciates, exporters are disadvantaged. If it is a long term deflation, say 3 to 30 years, exporting companies will suffer throughout the long term deflation. However, with a low exchange rate of the U.S. dollar, prices are cheaper and people's lives are better.

A high U.S. dollar exchange rate is often perceived by the public as better. It is a simple idea that better exports are better for the national economy. While this may be true in the early stages of a country's economic development or when the economy is struggling, it's not true when the benefits of economic growth are more evenly distributed.

Nowadays, when automation allows large companies to expand their factories, it doesn't have the same trickle-down effect as it used to because the automation doesn't even create 50% of the employment.

It is true that exports do well when the US dollar exchange rate is high. However, small and medium-sized enterprises and people become poorer due to more expensive raw materials and higher prices. Only a few people know that these profits, which are made more expensive by the US dollar exchange rate, are slowly transferred to large companies.

This is the hidden story. The exchange rate gains from an appreciating U.S. dollar are transferred from small businesses and people to large corporations.

If this policy of high US dollar exchange rate continues for even 10 years, the people and small and medium-sized enterprises will be poorer because the gains from the exchange rate appreciation will be transferred to the export co-n glomerates for free.

Naturally, income polarization will lead to weak domestic demand. Income polarization is furthered by the fact that income is skewed towards a few exporting companies and a few employees of those companies.

In every country, small and medium-sized enterprises employ the majority of the workforce, meaning that small and medium-sized enterprises employ three to four times as many people as large enterprises, a situation that could be exacerbated by a prolonged period of high US dollar exchange rates.

This, coupled with the fact that small and medium-sized enterprises offer lower wages and fewer benefits than large enterprises and the rising cost of living, makes it doubly difficult for ordinary people to make ends meet.

In this way, economic policy is directly connected to people's lives. Large corporations may welcome a high US dollar exchange rate, but they can't turn a blind eye to the deficits of small businesses forever.

This means that small and medium-sized enterprises are

forced to increase their delivery prices because they are operating on thin margins and eventually go out of business. and the unit price increase makes them uncompetitive in the export market. There's an uproar that exports are becoming uncompetitive.

So governments may decide to devalue their currencies against the US dollar. This reduces the amount of exports, but the people benefit from lower import prices.

In the case of long-term deflation, if the U.S. dollar depreciation lasts for more than a decade, the exchange rate gains of the exporting conglomerates will turn into exchange rate losses due to the depreciation, which will be shifted to the exporting conglomerates.

This is what Japan's lost 20 years meant: the collapse of Japan's export-oriented manufacturing conglomerates and a significant decline in international competitiveness.

Conversely, Japan's small and medium-sized enterprises have become powerful and have created many of the world's hidden champions.

However, for small and medium-sized enterprises without technology that simply rely on price competitiveness, the benefits of the low exchange rate are limited to lower import costs for raw materials and components.

They may even find it harder to sell their exports because of the lower price of the US dollar.

Only technological development can save them. This artificial US dollar exchange rate policy is equal to forcing a division between beneficiaries and non-beneficiaries. It can also be seen that a gradual decline in the exchange

Chapter 7)

Causes of Long Term Deflation (2)Population decline

In Japan, the core working-age population began to decline in 1990, and six years later, in 1996, the working-age population began to decline.

In Korea, the core working-age population began to decline in 2013, so demographically speaking, 2013 is the year that Korea's long term deflation began. In Japan, the long term deflation started in 1990 when the core working age population began to decline.

Six years later, in 2018, Korea's working-age population also began to shrink. However, Korea's long term deflation is stronger and faster than Japan's. The reason is the composition of the population. The reason for this is the composition of the population.

When large populations are close in age, they tend to have a large impact on the economy as they grow and retire. Japan and South Korea had baby booms after World War II.

South Korea's baby boomers (born between 1955 and 1963, 7.2 million people) are only 400,000 younger in absolute numbers than Japan's Dankai generation (born between 1947 and 1949, 6.8 million people).

As a percentage of the total population, South Korea's Baby Boomers are 2.5 times larger than Japan's Dankai generation. As a percentage of the total population, Japan's Dankai generation is one-third smaller at 5.7% than South Korea's baby boomers at 14.4%.

If you do the math, and if you consider population to be the biggest source of deflation, as Harry Dent argues, this means that South Korea's inflation is 2.5 times faster than Japan's deflation.

In South Korea, this means that the side effects of Japan's lost 30 years can be seen in just 12 years. Japan has a population of 120 million, about 2.5 times larger than Korea's 50 million.

Even the long term deflationary phenomenon is also worrisome because it will happen quickly. In short, it is fair to say that Korea faces a sharper long term deflation than Japan.

We believe that Korea is past the point of a 30-50% asset market bubble, just like Japan in 1989. So from now on, there will be no place to invest like in Japan.

Wealth that is not prepared in advance is transferred to others. To avoid being a victim of unintentional wealth transfer, I recommend that everyone read my first book on long term deflation two or three times.

This book is the only book in the world to study long term deflation in earnest, and I believe it's the only book in the world that does so

For a while, Harry Dent's population cliff was the talk of the town. Many people misunderstood it to mean that the working-age population (people aged 15 to 64) is shrinking and we can't make things.

However, in the author's opinion, long term deflation is not caused by a shrinking working age population. The lack of working-age people can be easily replaced by automation or female labor.

And now we have AI. People between the ages of 15 and 64 are called the working age, which, if you flip it around, is also the working age of consumption.

In other words, don't be fooled into thinking that the global economy is headed for deflation simply because there are fewer people of working age. The world is not deflationary because of a lack of production, but because of a lack of consumption.

The lack of production can be easily solved by automation with AI robots. The new social activities of women that increase production and consumption at the same time are much more important than automation through machines. Women's new social activities, such as housewives, increase production and consumption at the same time.

Therefore, the cause of deflation should be viewed from

the perspective of underconsumption.

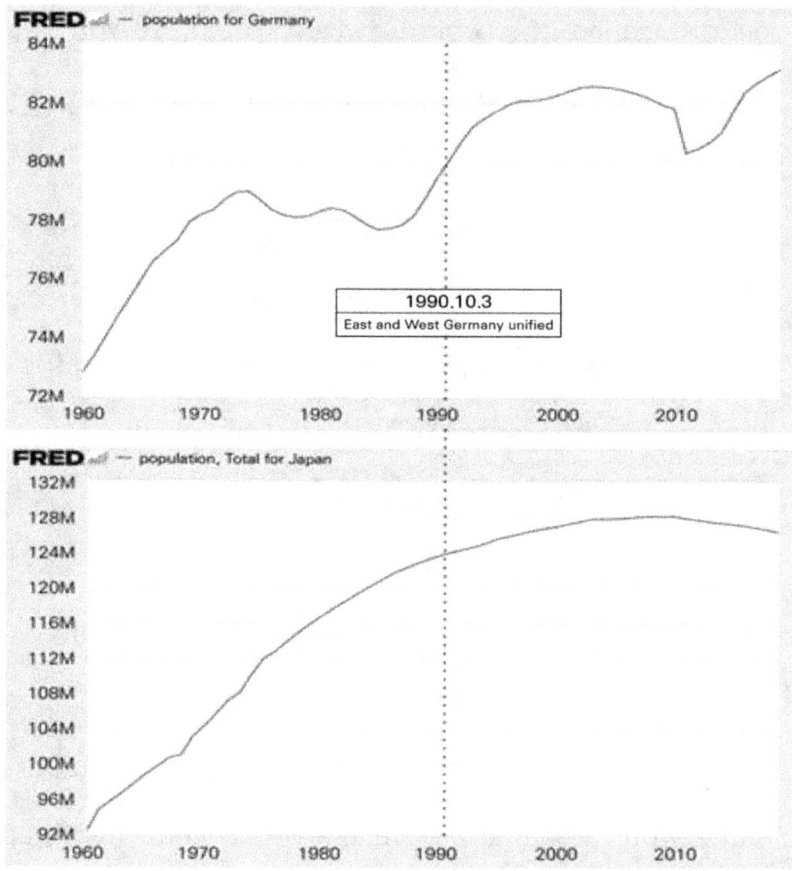

[Fig.10] Graph of total population in Germany and Japan in the same year and month (1960.1.1. to 2019.1.1.)

Back in the days when Malthusian demography ruled the world, Deng Xiaoping proclaimed that "population is an asset". The time has come for this to be true. Population is important for any country, and it cannot be increased in a short period of time.

In pre-unification Germany, where there was once talk of the country's demise, the unification of East and West Germany led to a population explosion. The population of about 12 million people in East Germany was quickly merged into a unified Germany.

Consider the graph of the total population of Germany and Japan in the same year and month (1960.1.1. to 2019.1.1.) in [Figure 10]. On October 3, 1990,

Germany was reunified and the total population increased by about 12 million people overnight, and then the German disappearance theory disappeared completely. Population has become so important.

With the exception of the U.S. in the 1930s, Japan was

the only country in the world in long term deflation until it escaped in 2020.

Harry Dent argues that the reason for the sudden decline in Japan's working-age population is the retirement of the Dankai generation.

Now that the Dankai generation is all retired and has little income other than pensions, it makes sense that they would reduce production and consumption.

We're not going to go into deflation right away as Harry Dent fears, because the Dankai generation in Japan or the baby boomers in Korea aren't going to disappear off the face of the earth, they're just going to spend a little less because they're earning less.

In other words, Harry Dent is over insightful.
In contrast, the decline in the price of the dollar is more

immediate and indiscriminate than the decline in consumption due to population decline. It is reasonable to assume that the decline in consumption demand due to population decline is reflected slowly and at a smaller rate.

[Fig.11] Trends in the exchange rate of the yen and the mark to the dollar in the same year after the Plaza Accord (1971.1 - 2001.1.2.)

Therefore, it is fair to say that the analysis of long term

deflation as an immediate consequence of population decline is somewhat overstated.

The declining birthrate and aging population in the world's major economies will also play a role in the long term deflationary forces.

Next, let's compare the exchange rate of the yen and the mark to the dollar after the Plaza Accord of September 22, 1985. We can see that there is no significant difference between Japan and Germany.

In other words, we can infer that it was not the exchange rate difference that caused the situation in Japan and Germany to reverse sharply, but the population problem.

In Germany, the sharp drop in the exchange rate of the mark to the dollar would have generated a strong deflationary force of price decline, but the population, or consumption, increased significantly, so that the theory of state disappearance disappeared completely.

[Figure 11] is a graph comparing the price trend of the Japanese yen and the German mark on the same date from January 1971 to January 2, 2001.

Chapter 8)

Causes of Long Term Deflation (3)Overindebtedness

Among the causes of long term deflation, the next thing to think about is the overindebtedness of governments, individuals, and corporations. This is the problem of overindebtedness. When there is a lot of debt, economic entities are naturally hindered in their consumption activities.

As shown in [Figure 7], the yen-dollar exchange rate has been falling almost continuously since 1971. In April 1990, when Japan's long term deflation began in earnest, the yen-dollar rate was 158.85 won. Twenty-five years later, in January 2012, it dropped by 64% to a low of 76.34 yen.

In more detail, Japan entered long term deflation in

December 1988 and remained in long term deflation until December 2020, 32 years later, with the yen-dollar exchange rate dropping 64% in 25 years. In simple terms, this means that import prices dropped by 64% on average.

The world entered long term deflation in January 2016. The author believes that Japan has exited long term deflation after 32 years. Looking at Japan, he believes that the world's long term deflation could continue until 2048.

This is because we believe that the world's long term deflation could last as long as Japan's, which is 32 years. In 2023, the world will be in the eighth year of long term deflation, which is already eight years old.

If the long term deflation lasts for 32 years, it will end in 2016 + 32 = 2048. That leaves 2048-2023=25 years.

South Korea has about 2.5 times more working-age people as a percentage of the total population than Japan. This suggests that Korea's long term deflation is likely to be 2.5 times faster than Japan's.

This is where the " quickly, quickly" comes in. Korea has 32/2.5=12.8, or about 13 more years, and 2016+13= 2029, which means that the long term deflation will end in 2029 and the economy will return to normal.

In other words, if the whole world except Korea goes through a long term deflationary period like Japan, it is very likely that the whole world except Korea will be in a long term deflationary state for about 25 years.

The global long term deflation will only end in 2023, 25 years from now, in 2048. South Korea exits long term deflation around 2029.

This is also indirect evidence that the rest of the world, with the exception of Japan, will be depreciating against the dollar by 2029 for Korea and 2048 for the rest of the world. That's 25 more years of low interest rates, low inflation, low exchange rate (low dollar), and low growth.

The remaining long term deflationary period in Korea is 5 years. During this time, no one will survive the long term deflation period. There is nowhere to invest except in cash and government bond and one or two reversal commercial goods.

This is the phenomenon of long term deflation. This long term deflation lasts for 25 years.
So going forward, until 2029 in Korea and 2048 globally, the price of the dollar will continue to fall in every country in the world except Japan, so if you invest in

dollars, that is, you should never invest abroad.

During a long term deflation, the dollar is not a safe haven asset. Since the world is already in a long term deflation, the dollar is not a safe haven until 2029 in Korea and 2048 globally.

The absolute amount of debt is also a problem, and the type of mortgage is also a big factor. The three countries, Korea, China, and Japan, adopted the right of recourse style mortgage systems that leave little room for consumption. Debt can be divided into national debt, corporate debt, and individual debt.

South Korea's household debt is 102%. Corporate debt is also at 126.1% of GDP. The government debt ratio is also expected to rise to 55.2% in 2023.

There is a debate on whether or not to include

Jeonse(Korean House rental system) rental payments and public corporation debt in the total debt of each economic entity. Regardless, all three economic entities - households, corporations, and governments - are burdened by debt.

The biggest problem is household debt, and if we retroactively change to the US-style right of non-recourse mortgage system, the debt will be cleared at once and the economy will be revitalized.

However, if we continue with the right of recourse mortgage systems, which are simply debt deferral systems like Korea and Japan, we can only dream of returning to an inflationary economy after the natural attrition of debtors has occurred.

The right of recourse mortgage systems in the East, including China, Japan, and Korea, will continue to weigh on the economy.

If they want to participate in the real estate rises start around 2043, they'll have to reform their mortgage systems to be more Americanized. If debt is going to cause pain in people's lives, it should be short-lived.

The American-style debt settlement system that overcame the 2008 financial crisis in a short period of time will reduce people's suffering.

But an even bigger problem stands in the way: the population cliff. In short, there is little hope for South Korea and the rest of the world going forward. As a solution to deflation, Japan has adopted quantitative easing. It's called Abenomics. Deflation destroys big companies.

On the contrary, it revitalizes small and medium-sized

enterprises. It enriches individuals. It has the same effect as using a so-called low exchange rate policy.

As shown in [Figure 7], the Japanese yen has fallen from 360 yen in the 1970s to 72 yen in 2014, which is a simple calculation: import prices have dropped by 80% in 44 years.

In simple terms, everything in Japan has fallen by 80% in 44 years, simply in proportion to the spike in the value of the yen. Short term deflation, which we usually experience every decade or so, is a temporary drop in asset prices, but they usually recover in two to three years, just like they always do.

However, long term deflation is a continuous decline in asset prices for at least 10 years, usually 5 to 30 years or more. Therefore, if we do not distinguish between short term deflation and long term deflation, the wealth of the existing rich will be destroyed and transferred to others, and finally new wealth will be created.

Next is the debt of each government.
Compared to the GDP of each country, the United States is 121%, Japan is 248%, and South Korea is 55%. Next is the debt of individuals.

South Korea is 104%, Japan is 60%, and the US is 76%. Corporate debt is also important. US companies have a debt-to-GDP ratio of 76%, South Korea 126%, and Japan 119%. Japan is number one in national debt, and South Korea is number one in household and corporate debt.

If these debts are not repaid, it will be difficult to revive the economy. Furthermore, the mortgage system, which accounts for the majority of individual debt, differs significantly between the United States and other countries. The U.S. has a non-recourse mortgage system, while China and Japan have a recourse mortgage system.

The difference between non-recourse and recourse is that in the U.S., if you borrow money against your home, the debt is considered repaid as soon as you vacate the home and hand over the keys to the bank, regardless of whether the value of the collateral has fallen or risen, and the bank has full recourse to the borrower's other assets. In these three countries, debt is also inherited.

When it comes to economic recovery, a non-recourse system makes it easier for the economy to survive. The system where the debt is canceled the moment the house is vacated and the keys are handed over to the bank, like in the United States, is a system that can revive the economy in a short period of time, although the temporary shock to the economy is large. It can be said to be an advanced system.

After 32 years of long term deflation, Japan has now emerged from long term deflation and normalized its economy. Japan's escape from long term deflation has many lessons.

However, neither banks nor governments will lend money if they expect to be unable to repay their debts, so the U.S. and Japanese solutions in 2008 and the coronavirus crisis have their limits. The value of collateral is declining, and there is no collateral at all. Banks have reached the limit of credit creation.

Debt cannot be reduced unless it is repaid. In order to repay the debt, i.e., the government bonds issued by the state, it is necessary to consider selling unnecessary state-owned property to pay off the debt. Someday, when the country's economy is stronger, it can buy back the property it sold if it needs it again.

It is natural that the debt ratio would decrease on its own if the productivity of the country's GDP increased dramatically by utilizing AI robots. However, since the current long term deflation is more due to a lack of consumption than a lack of production, this method has its limitations.

There is not much data on the long term deflation in the United States that began in 1929, or more precisely, in 1927. However, the Great Depression of the 1920s in the United States seems to have been caused by the bursting of a land speculation bubble that was triggered by a surge in the money supply.

Florida's land speculation and housing bubble burst after the U.S. government raised interest rates to curb stock speculation.

Land speculation in Miami Beach reached such a peak

that within two or three years, land that was worth $800 was selling for $150,000 in 1924. From 1924 to 1925, the real estate bubble reached its peak and began to collapse in 1926.

As the bubble collapsed, speculators were forced to pay off their debts. By 1927, Miami's real estate offices were almost all closed. It then became the city with the most bank failures in 1928 and 1929.

Unusually, land speculation occurred first, around 1924, and then shifted to stock speculation between 1927 and 1929. [Fig. 4]

The long-term graph of the Dow (1914-1968) shows that the Dow started its crash from 155 in 1927 to 362.35 on October 29, 1929.

The destructive power of the bubble was enormous

because credit was available for purchases, whether land or stocks, with only a 10% deposit.

[Figure 6] The graph of the Dow Jones Industrial Average shows that in June 1932, the Dow had fallen by 87.1% to 46.68. We can assume that land and housing prices would have dropped by the same percentage due to the diamond dollar investment method described earlier.

The actual bottom of the Dow was 46.68 in June 1932, but the timing of the start of the Great Rebound is slightly different depending on your perspective.

After hitting the lowest point of the Great Depression, the Dow rose considerably during World War II (1939.9.1. to 1945.9.2.), as shown in the long term graph of the Dow (1914-1968) in Figure 3.

The Dow graph also shows that economic growth

stagnated for about five years after the end of World War II.

Therefore, it is reasonable to consider the breakout of 203.46 in February 1950 as a turning point, i.e., the U.S. economy was barely beginning to recover its normal state 22 years after the bubble burst.

Coincidentally, June 25, 1950 was the day the Korean War broke out. The recovery of the U.S. economy may have had something to do with the Korean War, as there was a special war supply program.

Although people still refer to 1929 as the Great Depression, the author believes that the U.S. Great Depression of 1929 should actually be reclassified as the first long term deflation in history.

To be precise, the long term deflation of 1929 can be

assumed to have escaped due to the outbreak of the Korean War on June 25, 1950, which resulted in the repayment of debt and the reduction of the debt ratio due to the increase in income caused by the huge increase in output, i.e., the increase in GDP.

So far, we have discussed the main causes and effects of long term deflation using the Dow as an example. Now, let's take a look at how to recognize the signs of long term deflation, i.e., what economic indicators or data can be used to diagnose it.

Until now, no economic research institutes, professors, economists, or securities firms have properly studied long term deflation, so it is safe to say that the definition, causes, and countermeasures of long term deflation have been studied by few except the author.

Next, the practicalization of AI robots and the arrival of

a world of superconductors will also contribute to long term deflation. Tesla is the leader in humanoid robots. Tesla Bot is a humanoid robot called Optimus.

Through AI learning, the Tesla bot will be able to develop almost as fast as a human in terms of capabilities, which is faster than a child can grow. Optimus, the Tesla bot, could replace all human labor.

It seems that Tesla has been the leader of this business cycle. If so, it is almost self-evident that, according to the leading stock theory, Tesla's stock price will drop by 80-90% from its peak price, which means that the full bottom will be around $30-50 per share.

This is because the behavior of the stock price will be the same in Korea and the United States according to the leading stock theory.

Investors are all waiting for Tasla's stock price to drop, thinking they'll buy it when it does. However, according to the theory of leading stock investing, this is the wrong way to invest.

The probability of a once-leading stock returning to leadership in the next cycle is only 12.5%, based on a 53 year analysis of the Dow Jones Industrial Average. In other words, it's much more likely that Tasla will never return to leadership again.

If Tesla does return to the top, it will only happen if Optimus, the humanoid robot, makes a spectacular reappearance on the trading floor, creating new demand that has been missing.
In other words, Tesla will never be a leader in electric cars again.

In the future, the rise of humanoids could lead to a

revolution in domestic work and production, where labor costs would be zero. This means that in the long term, the production cost of all products will converge towards zero.

The direct and indirect labor cost of all products is around 50%. This means that the prices of all products and goods could drop by up to 50%.

Moreover, the long term deflationary effects of humanoid robots replacing human labor are permanent. This could lead to a shocking situation that surpasses the Luddite movement after the Industrial Revolution.

Due to the author's lack of technical knowledge, the long term deflationary effects of humanoid robots are listed in order of priority 4, but at the current rate of development of Tesla bots, the development of the robotics industry should be higher on the list of reasons for long term deflation.

These four reasons are the reasons why long term deflation will definitely be in full swing in the future, and humanity cannot avoid long term deflation in the ultra-long term. Therefore, the end of long term deflation is a long way off. I think the end of long term deflation will be around 2048.

If long term deflation is going to hit this hard and last this long, it becomes a no-brainer that you, the reader, as an investor, should be the first to recognize it and invest accordingly.

Finally, the discovery of superconductors. This will allow for a dramatic reduction in production costs. The cost of electricity, or energy, becomes about half the cost of all products, so the price of all goods crashes.

So, the causes of long term deflation around the world can be summarized as the long term weakness of the dollar, depopulation, excessive debt, the rise of humanoid robots, and the discovery and commercialization of superconductors.

Chapter 9)

Catching the Deflationary Moment

-In individual countries

First of all, deflation can be divided into short-term deflation and long term deflation depending on its duration. Furthermore, there are two types of deflation: those that occur only in one country and long term deflation that occurs worldwide.

First, let's briefly summarize the classification of deflation. As I mentioned earlier, the United States classifies deflation, i.e. a recession, as negative GDP growth for two consecutive quarters.

1)The classification method is different of long term deflation and short term deflation.

An indicator of whether an economy is in short term deflation is whether stock prices move inversely to the dollar. It's surprisingly simple.

In a short term deflation, i.e. a generalized deflation, the price of the dollar goes up and the price of stocks and apartments goes down inversely. So, the trick to spot the signs of short term deflation is to check whether the Diamond Dollar Investment Method is working properly or not. Think of the cyclical recessions we've all experienced.

Therefore, if you think that the Won to dollar exchange rate, i.e. the price of the dollar, will increase due to interest rate hikes, self-reflation, financial crisis, etc.

Six months after such an event, you should also sell your apartment. As a Korean investor, we should be able to recall the IMF, the 2008 financial crisis, the corona crisis, etc. that we have experienced.

The inverse relationship between the domestic dollar price of a country and its stock index, apartments, gold, crude oil, etc. is the Diamond Dollar Investment Method, which the author advocated long ago.

This investment method takes advantage of the fact that in any country except the United States, the rate of increase and decrease of the domestic dollar price is always the same as the individual rate of increase and decrease of all properties in that country. It also takes advantage of the fact that they are always inversely proportional to each other.

2) Whether a country is entering long term deflation is determined by whether the dollar and stocks move in the same direction according to the Diamond Dollar Method.

If the dollar and stocks are moving in the same direction, i.e. following the inverted diamond dollar method, then the country is in a long term deflation. This is also very easy to recognize.

The way to recognize a long term deflation is to determine that the economy has entered a long term deflation when the Diamond Dollar investing method does not work at all.

In a long term deflation, the price of stocks, apartments, gold, etc. and the price of the dollar become directly proportional instead of inversely proportional.

In long term deflation, the dollar price, stock prices, and apartment prices move in the same direction, but they all move in the direction of collapse.

Let's first look at how closely these three indicators, i.e.

the yen-dollar exchange rate and the Nikkei, housing index, have moved in the past in Japan, which exited long term deflation in 2020 with Abenomics, through a synchronization graph.

[Figure 12] shows the synchronization rate of the yen-dollar price, the Nikkei index, and the housing index in Japan from 2009 to 2019 (11 years), with three graphs of the same year in one graph.

At first glance, you can see that the behavior of these three indicators is strikingly similar. Therefore, the investment method for long term deflation, which will be explained later, is also based on analyzing the synchronization rate graph [Figure 12].

The following conclusions are drawn by application. We can see from [Figure 2] that Japan's long term deflation started in December 1988. This is after the vertical dotted line BC'②.

In the graph of the housing index at the bottom of [Figure 2], where the housing index starts to be displayed and the relationship with house prices can be examined at the same time, the yen-dollar price and the Nikkei index of the same year after point "D" are compared simultaneously with the housing index.

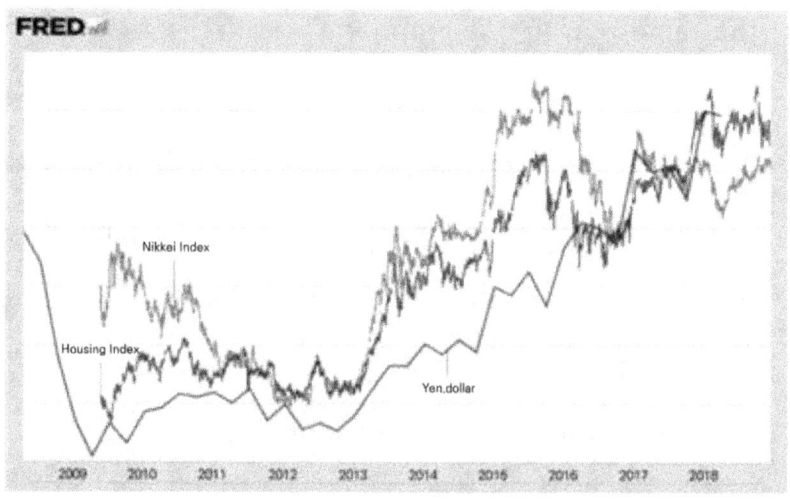

[Fig.12] Synchronization rate of yen and Nikkei housing index during Japan's long term deflation (2009-2019)

The vertical dotted lines ③, ④, and (5) in [Figure 2]

show the relationship between the value of the yen, the Nikkei index, and the housing index simultaneously.

Look at the synchronization rate of the three assets, i.e., the yen-dollar exchange rate graph, the Nikkei index, and the Japan Housing Index! You can see that the three graphs look similar.

In conclusion, this graph shows that when the dollar price goes down, stock and apartment prices go down, and when the dollar price goes up, stock prices go up, and apartment prices go up, in a long term deflation, and we can see from the graphs of the three data from 2009 to 2019 in Japan for about 11 years.

This fact is completely opposite to the common sense, i.e. the Diamond dollar investment method. This is the most important conclusion.

This is not the view of classical economists, nor of economists at the Institute of Economic Affairs. This argument is original to the author, i.e., we should never forget the surprising fact that in countries with long term deflation, the direction of the domestic dollar price is the same as the direction of the price of stocks, apartments, gold, silver, etc.

This is the most important, strongest, and only evidence that you should be especially careful when investing during long term deflation. When a country is in the midst of a long term deflation, the relationship between the dollar's exchange rate and all property in that country becomes directly proportional, not inversely proportional as in normal times.

Of course, various commodities also move in the same direction as the dollar exchange rate, so it is very easy for companies and investors to take advantage of this situation to decide whether to buy commodities.

Therefore, each economic entity should determine when the direction of the dollar and the direction of the movement of stocks, apartments, and major commodities become the same, and the beginning of long term deflation will be found.

The graph above [Fig. 12] shows a rough comparison of the yen-dollar exchange rate in Japan for about 11 years from 2009 to 2019, the change of the Nikkei index according to the price change of the yen-dollar exchange rate, and the change of the Japanese housing index according to the change of the yen-dollar exchange rate in the same year.

You can see the behavior of each over an 11-year period.
While the three graphs are roughly similar, they look

much more similar after 2012, i.e., the synchronization rate has increased significantly. 2012 was the first year of Abenomics, so it seems that Abe's economic policies, which he took over as prime minister in December 2012, began to take effect.

In other words, when long term deflation starts, you have to completely reverse the way you have been investing in dollars and assets.

Instead of investing in an inverse relationship between the dollar and local assets, you need to invest in a direct relationship. This evidence is one of the authors' most revealing arguments.

[Fig.12] shows that Abenomics was on the right track in its attempt to escape long term deflation. We will see in [Chapter 15] that Abenomics eventually brought Japan out of long term deflation.

The direction of Abenomics was the right one, even though we learned from the actions of the US FRB Chairman Bernanke after the 2008 subprime crisis and the 2020 coronavirus crisis.

This is the solution to long term deflation that only the author has found after nearly 30 years, during which no one knew the solution to long term deflation, which is to pump money into the market indefinitely. In conclusion, Abenomics, which aims to reduce the value of the yen, has been a great success.

But,
the inflationary side effect of money printing is a side effect. The duration of inflation is prolonged, the inflation rate is higher than before, and the period of high interest rates is extended.

In countries with long term deflation, i.e., except for Japan, which is in short term deflation, investors who are used to the old days of inflation, i.e., the days of short term deflation, when you could get rich just by holding real estate or stocks for a long period of time, will find that in about 30 years, their property has fallen to 10-20% of the current price.

By analyzing why this happens, we can find ways to combat long term deflation. From this, we realize that during a long term deflation, investors need to follow a completely different investment approach than they do during a short term deflation, i.e., they need to invest differently. In a nutshell, the only answer is to invest in the inverse diamond dollar method! is the only answer.

The goal of this book is to help you avoid investments that will crash and burn over time and instead find investments that will grow your wealth 8x or more. The reason for analyzing the causes of long term deflation is also to properly inform readers about financial technology, i.e. fintech.

Since 2009, the price of the dollar, the Nikkei, and the Japanese housing index have all been rising in Japan. In a normal economy, the price of the dollar should rise and the price of stocks and real estate commodities should fall.

However, as shown in [Fig.12], the long term deflation is still ongoing in 2019, so the dollar price is rising, stocks are rising, and real estate is rising, which is a strange phenomenon.

Abenomics is all about driving the yen down, and the yen-dollar has been at 140 yen since 2023. It is currently at 150 yen. Japan exits long term deflation in December 2020, i.e. after ④ in [Fig.27].

To capture long term deflation in detail, it is necessary to distinguish between a country-specific case and a global case.

The first way to detect the onset of long term deflation in a certain country is to look for the time when the relationship between the dollar exchange rate and the stock index of the country starts to stop being determined by the Diamond Dollar Investment Method, i.e. when the inverse relationship between the dollar exchange rate and the stock index changes to a direct relationship.

Next, you can look at the relationship with the housing index, but some countries don't publish housing indexes every year, and some don't even publish housing indexes at all, so you might have to rely on the relationship with the stock index.

The vertical dotted lines ② and ③ in [Fig.2] explain this.

The vertical dotted line ② is the normal investment method, the Diamond Dollar Investment Method.

The graph shows that if you apply the Diamond Dollar Investment Method after ②, you will lose a lot of money. In this section, the dollar goes up, stock prices go up, and apartments go up. [Fig.19] further confirms that the Diamond Dollar Investment Method does not apply at all.

[Figure 2] is a graph that corresponds the changes in the Japanese yen and the Nikkei index over a long period of 48 years with the changes in the Japanese housing index in the same month of the same year, and their relationship to each other.

[Fig.12] shows the change in the Nikkei index and the change in house prices in response to the change in the yen exchange rate over a period of about 11 years (2009-2019).

It is unfortunate that the BIS (Bank of International Settlements) does not provide graphs of the Nikkei index and the housing index for the same period prior to 2009, so it is not possible to analyze the changes in the Nikkei index and the housing index over the 48 years of yen-dollar fluctuations.

This is why we take a closer look at [Fig.19], which shows a simultaneous comparison of the yen-dollar, the Nikkei index, and the housing index from 2009 to 2019, when the housing index became available. We can see that the inverse relationship between the dollar and the other indicators has changed to a proportional relationship.

It is unclear whether the dollar is rising due to short term deflation or the price of the dollar rising even in normal times, causing stock prices to fall, or whether the dollar is rising due to foreign exchange demand such as foreigners who sold their stocks, but the results show that the dollar and stock indexes go in opposite directions.

If at some point they are in the same direction, we are now moving from short term deflation to long term deflation.
As you can see in sections 2 and 3 of [Figure 2], the dollar is rising and stock prices are rising at the same rate.

It is clear that we need to look at the movements of the exchange rate and stocks, i.e. the direction of the trend, rather than one or two days.

If you look at the behavior of both in Japan in the 1980s, you can see that the stock index was on a major upswing, but at some point, i.e. around December 1988, the price of the dollar continued to rise even as the stock index continued to rise.

This is the beginning of long term deflation.
This is the most characteristic phenomenon of long term deflation. What is surprising is that contrary to popular belief, the long term deflation had already started about a year before the stock market crash, i.e. the Great Crash, but no one realized this.

We emphasize once again that the beginning of long term deflation is when the conventional Diamond Dollar Investment Method starts to be applied in reverse, i.e. where the reverse Diamond Dollar Investment Method starts to be applied is where long term deflation starts.

From December 1988 until January 4, 1990, when the Nikkei Stock Average began its general decline, both the stock index and the domestic dollar price continued to rise sharply. Then, on January 4, 1990, both the dollar price and the Nikkei began to fall sharply.

Again, since the Japanese real estate index for the period is not available, we cannot confirm the exact relationship between the real estate price and the dollar price and the stock index, but we can infer that it was moving in the same direction and width as the Nikkei index with a lag of about 5 months according to the Diamond dollar investment method.

Since the Japanese housing index has been available since 2010, we cannot directly check the movement of Japanese real estate on the graph, but we can infer this by looking at point D in [Figure 2], i.e. the movement of the Japanese housing index since July 2009.

After one business cycle, it is not reasonable to see a difference in returns between investment assets, because money is driven by the profit motive and moves to the most profitable place. Therefore, in the long term, the growth rate of the two major investment assets, stocks and real estate, is almost the same.

So, when the great bubble bursting of stocks and apartments, which is expected to hit the world in June and December 2021, begins, it is important to distinguish whether it will be a short term or long term deflationary phenomenon.

Only time will tell, but for those of us in the financial space, there is a lot of money to be made in anticipation. The reason is that investing in short term deflation is completely different from investing in long term deflation.

The reason why we can think that the economic fluctuation that will come after the change in the KOSPI index and the dollar price in 2021 is a short term deflation, i.e. a normal recession, is that the Japanese Plaza Accord caused the yen to surge by about 33.3% from 240 yen to 160 yen in just one day.

Many experts are now predicting that the price of the dollar will slowly decline by another 30-40% in the future. The relevance of the Diamond Dollar Investment Method can be easily demonstrated by looking at the IMF in Korea, Brexit in the UK, the inverse relationship between the dollar, crude oil, and gold prices in [Figure 13], the graph of the dollar index and international gold prices in [Figure 14], and the 36-year relationship between the Japanese yen, dollar, Nikkei, and housing index in [Figure 27].

Since December 1988, the direction of the Japanese yen, the direction of the Nikkei, and the direction of the Nikkei index have moved in the same direction. This is the phenomenon of long term deflation.

Until now, no one has realized this fact, and the author has ingeniously analyzed this phenomenon using data provided by FRED and demonstrated it through long term graphs.

Since January 2016, the Korean dollar price and the KOSPI index, the country's main stock index, have been moving in almost the same direction, indicating that long term deflation is in full swing in Korea.

From this point on, you need to completely change your financial strategy. other words, it is important to keep in mind that even after the main bull market is over, you should not replace the dollar you invested in during the short term deflation.

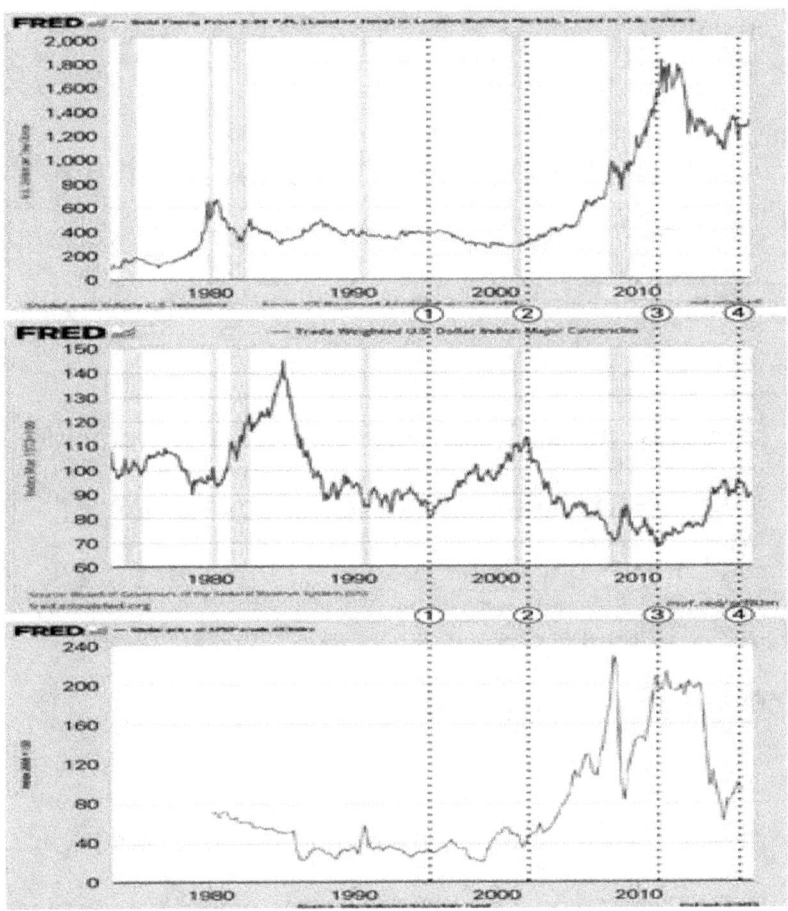

[Fig.13] The inverse relationship of the dollar to crude oil and gold prices

This is because when the KOSPI index falls, the price of

the dollar will also fall and vice versa, i.e. if you follow the Diamond Dollar Investment Method like a short term deflation, it will be a backward-looking investment.

This means that you should not invest in dollars at home or abroad for about 20 years or more, i.e., you should not hold dollar cash or make dollar deposits at home.

Don't just think, 'I don't have any dollars,' but under the dollar reserve currency system, everyone uses dollars to send money out of the country to invest or bring it back into the country, so if you have invested overseas, it is the same as having dollars.

In the future, the domestic dollar will gradually fall below 860 won, so the money invested overseas by Korean citizens is also destined to become a ghost dollar.

Therefore, the curse of the won will gradually appear in

Korea just like the curse of the yen.

In general, the best way to make money in a short term deflation is to hold cash. But outside the U.S., the dollar is not an investment at all in a long term deflation.

The dollar is cash for U.S. residents in the U.S., i.e., Americans can hold cash in the U.S. in short term deflation as a hedge against long term deflation.

But for the rest of the world, dollars are more like property than cash in a long term deflation, and as we've already discussed in detail, you should never hold dollars. It will crash. So the dollar is a monster.

Chapter 10)

Catching the Deflationary Moment

-In the whole world

It is determined by the relationship between the international gold price and the dollar index.

If it is inversely proportional, it is a short term deflationary state, and if it is proportional, it is a long term deflationary state.
In long term deflation, the relationship between the international gold price and the dollar index becomes a direct proportion. This is when global long term deflation begins.

[Figure 1] is a simple illustration of the Diamond Dollar Investment Method. As the price of the dollar changes, gold and crude oil find their equilibrium. This is a diagram of the process of finding an equilibrium between the dollar and assets through bubbles and counter-bubbles.

The vertical dotted line in [Figure 13] shows the inverse relationship between the Korean Won to dollar exchange rate and the prices of crude oil and gold on the same date, and in particular, if you look at the changes in the Won to dollar, gold, and crude oil, you can see that the prices of gold and crude oil move in the opposite direction to the dollar as the price of the dollar changes.

You can also see that gold is slightly more responsive to the dollar than crude oil. However, we can also see that crude oil eventually becomes inversely proportional to the dollar price.

The relationship between the dollar index, i.e. the

international price of the dollar, and the international price of crude oil can also be seen separately from gold in [Figure 19].

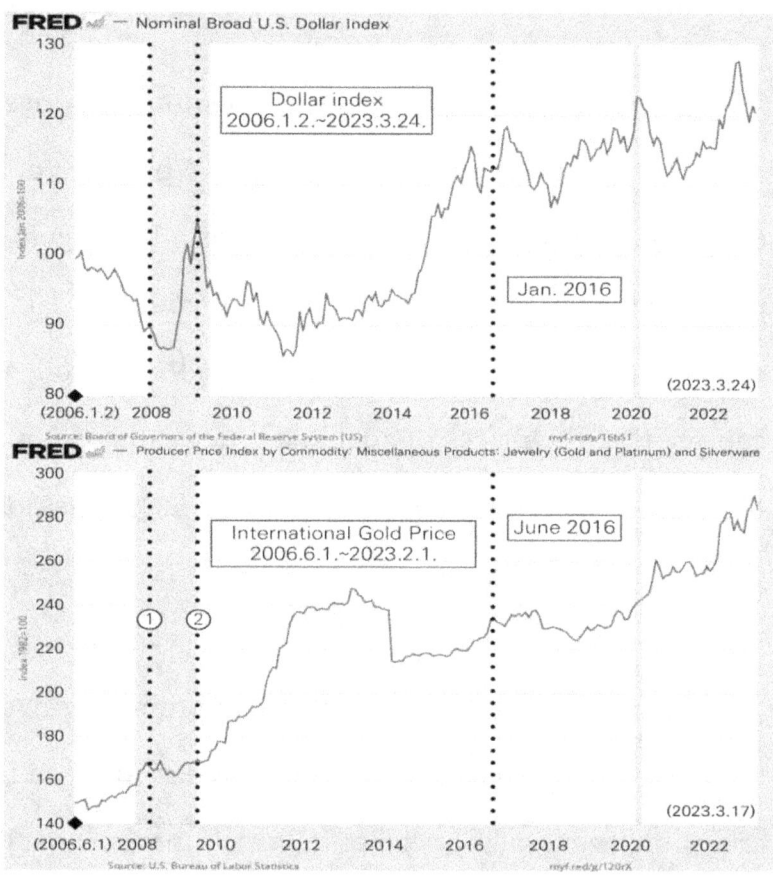

[Fig.14] Dollar Index and International gold prices (2006.1-2023.3)

Applying this to practical investments, you can invest in

gold, crude oil, and other international commodities knowing that the price of the dollar is inversely related to the price of all commodities, and if you invest accordingly, you can choose the right time and price to buy or sell.

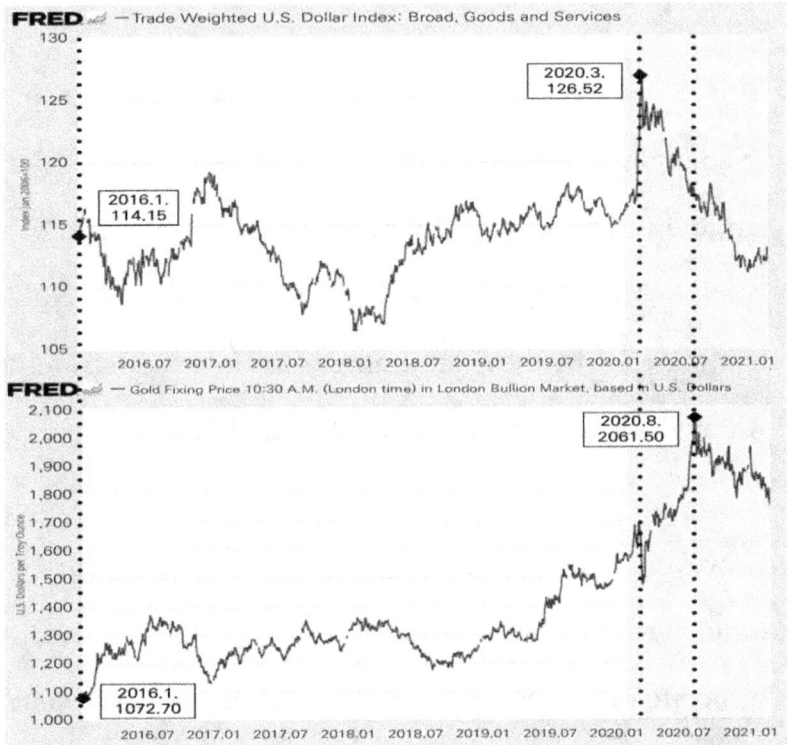

[Fig.15]Dollar Index and International Gold Price (2016.1.2.~2021.2.28.)

This fact is summarized in the Diamond Dollar Investment Method, which is a method for buying and selling assets according to the Diamond Dollar Investmnet Method. Outside of the U.S., this technique is applicable to any country and any time period.

This is a very important investment point, i.e. a falling exchange rate in any country indiscriminately triggers a surge in the prices of assets such as real estate and stocks. The opposite is also true. This principle is summarized in the Diamond Dollar Investment Method. An extension of this is the long term deflation theory.

However, it"s important to note that in a country with long term deflation, short term deflation, i.e., the opposite of the usual outcome of investing, will occur. Now let's get more specific

The vertical dotted line ④ in [Fig. 13] shows that until

now, the relationship between the gold price and the dollar was inversely proportional to each other according to the Diamond Dollar Investment Method. The vertical dotted line ④ is January 2016. After January 2016, the relationship between gold and the dollar is not inversely proportional but directly proportional.

Strictly speaking, [Figure 13] is a little insufficient to explain long term deflation because the middle figure is a graph of the Won to dollar exchange rate. However, it has the advantage of showing the relationship between the Won to dollar exchange rate and gold and crude oil at the same time.

You can see the long term deflationary situation in another figure. The relationship between the international dollar and international gold since January 2016 can be seen in the graphs in [Figure 14] and [Figure 15].

[Figure 15] is what we want to look at again after point ④ in [Figure 13], i.e., both graphs in [Figure 14] start on January 2, 2016, the same day as point ④ in [Figure 13]. The vertical dotted lines in the graphs are set to 2016.1.2. i.e., if you draw a vertical dotted line anywhere, you can see the international dollar price and international gold price on that date.

The author considers 2016.1.2. to be the start of the world's long term deflation, which makes January 2016 a very important tipping point.

In [Figure 15], we can see that the relationship between the international dollar price, the dollar index, and the international gold price has changed from the usual inverse relationship to a proportional relationship over a period of about six years, from January 2, 2016 to February 28, 2021. This is the only evidence that the world has entered a long term deflationary state.

Of course, Japan entered long term deflation in December 1988 and has been in long term deflation ever since. Therefore, after January 2016, the world is in a long term deflationary state.
The start date of the graph in [Figure 15] is January 2016.

The start of Japan's long term deflation was explained in [Figure 2] as the start of the proportional relationship between the domestic dollar and the Nikkei stock price, as shown in the vertical dotted lines ② and ③. The vertical dotted line BC'②, i.e. December 1988.

In other words, whether an individual country is entering long term deflation is determined by whether the country's stock index is inversely or directly proportional to the increase in the country's dollar exchange rate.

On the other hand, whether long term deflation is localized or globalized is determined by whether the price of international gold, an international commodity, and the price of the dollar index, an international dollar, are inversely or directly proportional.

The author concludes that the current long term deflation is inevitable for the entire world, especially Korea.

The inverse relationship between the international gold price and the dollar index is shown in [Fig. 14] and [Fig.15], and since January 2016, there has already been a global long term deflationary situation. Gold is an international commodity and the price difference between countries is mainly due to taxes and nothing else.

However, since this time, we can see that the international commodity gold price and the international dollar price, which should always be inversely proportional, have become directly proportional.

The first figure in [Figure 15] is a graph of the dollar index, and the second figure shows the price of international gold. The phenomenon of a direct relationship between the gold price and the dollar began to appear after ④ in [Figure 13]. [Figure 15] is a graph that confirms the situation after ④ in [Figure 13] for a longer term.

In Japan, where actual long term deflation began in December 1988, we can see from [Figure 2] that the dollar and the stock housing index have been moving in a direct proportional relationship since then, following the inverse Diamond dollar investment method (a phenomenon where the dollar moves in a direct proportional relationship with assets such as stocks and apartments).

[Fig.16] Gold price follows the trajectory of the dollar index price 5 months ago

The Minden graph in [Fig. 15] has been artificially time-lagged by about 5 months, i.e., matched, to the time when the dollar and gold peaked in [Fig. 16].

[Figure 16] confirms the author's claim, i.e., that the international dollar and international gold prices are inversely related in long term deflation, not directly related. In [Figure 16], the authors examine the trend of the dollar index price and the international gold price by arbitrarily aligning the peaks of the international dollar price and international gold price to the same date, ignoring the date of the peak.

The authors found a surprising phenomenon, i.e., the international dollar price, or the Dollar Index price, peaks five months after the international gold price peaks.

Prior to this, the Dollar Index and the international gold price were always trending in the same direction, but five months after the trajectory of the dollar price, the international gold price follows almost 100% closely the trajectory of the dollar price five months earlier.

This can be seen by simply noting that the peaks in the top and bottom graphs in [Figure 16] are about five months apart.

The vertical dotted lines in [Figure 16] are drawn arbitrarily to facilitate comparison, and we can also see the synchronization of the international dollar price with the international gold price. The top graph in [Figure 16] shows the international dollar price since January 2, 2016. The lower figure is a graph of the international gold price since June 2016.

The highest price of the dollar was 126.5236 in March

2020. The vertical dotted line is the © line, which shows this relationship at a glance. It is always important to remember that there is a lag of about 5 months between the peak in the international price of the dollar and the peak in the international price of gold.

In a long term deflationary situation, the international dollar price and the international gold price are directly proportional to each other. It's just that the international gold price moves later, with a trajectory that almost 100% mirrors the trajectory of the international dollar price five months later. The dollar moves first, and following the trajectory of the international dollar, gold moves along the same trajectory.

This fact gives investors two important takeaways.

First, it is possible to determine the arrival of

international long term deflation.

Secondly, when importing or selling gold internationally, you can invest according to the trajectory of the international price of the dollar five months ago.

The entire world, including Korea, has been in long term deflation since 2016. Of course, Japan was already in long term deflation before January 2016, long before the rest of the world entered long term deflation. However, Japan has been out of long term deflation for 32 years, and the world is now in temporary inflation.

The relationship between the US dollar index and the international gold price since January 2016, after (4) in [Figure 13], can be seen in [Figure 15].

[Figure 16] shows the relationship between the US dollar index and the international gold price from January 2006 to March 2023. It is important to note that the period adjustments at the bottom and top of Figure 16 have already been adjusted by 5 months.

[Figure 15] is a graph of the relationship between the Dollar Index and the international gold price without a period adjustment. [Figure 16] is a graph of the international gold price compared to the Dollar Index five months ahead.

In [Figure 16], we can see that the trajectory of the Dollar Index graph is followed by the international gold price about 5 months later.

By examining these graphs, it can be seen that before January 2016, the international price of the dollar and the international price of gold moved in an inverse relationship.

Similarly, after January 2016, the graphs show that the

dollar index and the international gold price are moving in the same direction, i.e. proportionally. We can use this to recognize an investment technique that almost always pays off by investing in gold internationally.

The way to detect long term deflation in an individual country is to compare the country's exchange rate to the dollar and the country's stock index. A way to recognize the arrival of long term deflation globally is based on when the international gold price begins to move in direct proportion to the dollar index.

This method of capturing long term deflation is original to the author. Until now, no one has separated deflation into short term and long term deflation, and no scholar or economic organization has recognized that they should be captured and treated differently.

Ben Bernanke's quantitative easing and other

deflation-fighting methods were born after his arrival as FED chairman. As a result, the world is now fighting a war against inflation.

In other words, we don't know the consequences of QE yet. The fight against inflation has always been a long and difficult process. This time around, the fight against inflation will be similarly long and arduous, with one simple phrase: Higher and Longer! in a nutshell.

I wonder if the hasty rate cuts will lead the world to a third wave of inflation, as usual, and we will have to face higher interest rates and inflation for a longer period of time.

Chapter 11)

Neither Korea nor the world can escape Japanese-style long term deflation.

As of 2023, South Korea's household and enterprise debt to GDP ratio is the highest in the world. In the 1980s, a triple-dip economic boom sparked a global real estate and stock speculation fever.

When Japan's economy suddenly slumped after the Plaza Accord of 1985 caused the yen to surge in value, the government eased lending restrictions to stimulate the economy and quickly brought down interest rates.

No one talks about it, but there's no more powerful deflationary force than a falling exchange rate. There is no more powerful deflationary force than currency declines. A depreciating exchange rate reduces the price of goods indiscriminately.

During the boom, Japan's Sony purchased the pride of America, Columbia Pictures, and Panasonic bought Universal Pictures. Japanese real estate conglomerates took over the Empire State Building, the symbol of New York.

In particular, when Rockefeller Center, a symbol of American capitalism, was taken over, Americans were so shocked that they said it was a second attack on Pearl Harbor. At the time, 70% of the world's billionaires were Japanese.

However, on January 4, 1990, about five years after the Plaza Accord in New York. As soon as the stock market opened, the Nikkei began to collapse.

Then, on January 4, 1990, real estate began to collapse. Many of the banks, insurance companies, and securities firms that were hit by the grenade went under as borrowers became insolvent, unable to repay their loans even if they sold their homes.

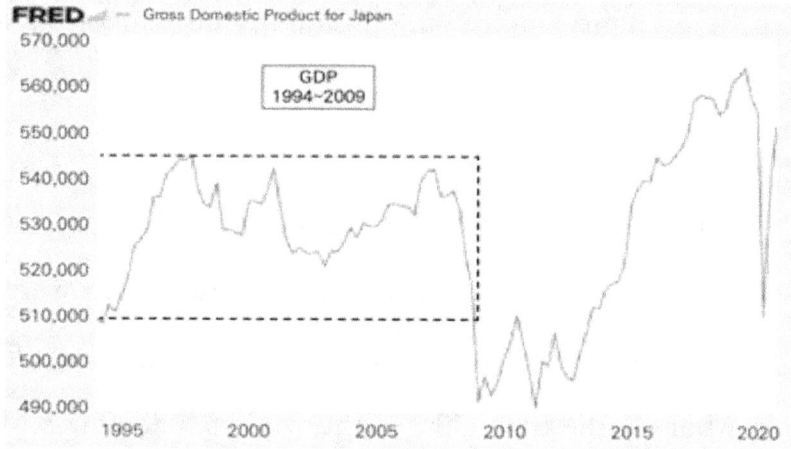

[Fig.17] GDP trends in Japan

As shown in [Figure 2], we can see that the Nikkei has collapsed by about 80-90% after a sharp rise. Moreover, what was thought to be a short term deflation, turned out to be a long term deflation for 32 years, leading to a long period of low growth, so stocks were thoroughly differentiated.

As shown in [Figure 4], the land index collapsed by about 90%. The land index before July 2009 cannot be compared to the 48-year graph of the yen-dollar exchange rate and the Nikkei index in [Figure 2] at the same time because the changes over the same period are not available, but it can be inferred that it could have dropped like the yen and the Nikkei index.

On the other hand, the value of the yen continued to rise. As a result, about $3.5 trillion of Japan's overseas investments became phantom dollars due to exchange losses, making it almost impossible to bring them back into the country.

As shown in [Fig. 17], Japan's GDP fluctuated in a range until the 2008 financial crisis. In the three lost decades since 1990, Japan's real average wage has been almost flat, increasing by only ¥180,000 (4.4%). Over the same period, South Korea's real wage increased about 1.9 times, actually overtaking Japan in 2015.

Looking at nominal GDP as reported by the IMF, over the past 30 years, China's nominal GDP has grown 37 times, the U.S. has grown 3.5 times, and Germany has grown 2.3 times, while Japan's has only grown 1.5 times due to the long term deflation that hit in 1990.

In 2016, long term deflation hit in full force, meaning that real wage growth and nominal GDP globally and in South Korea almost stop growing during long term deflation, i.e. 10 to 30 years, just like in Japan.

Japan's downfall is due to the continuous and relentless decline in the price of the dollar in Japan, the decline in the working age population, and government debt.

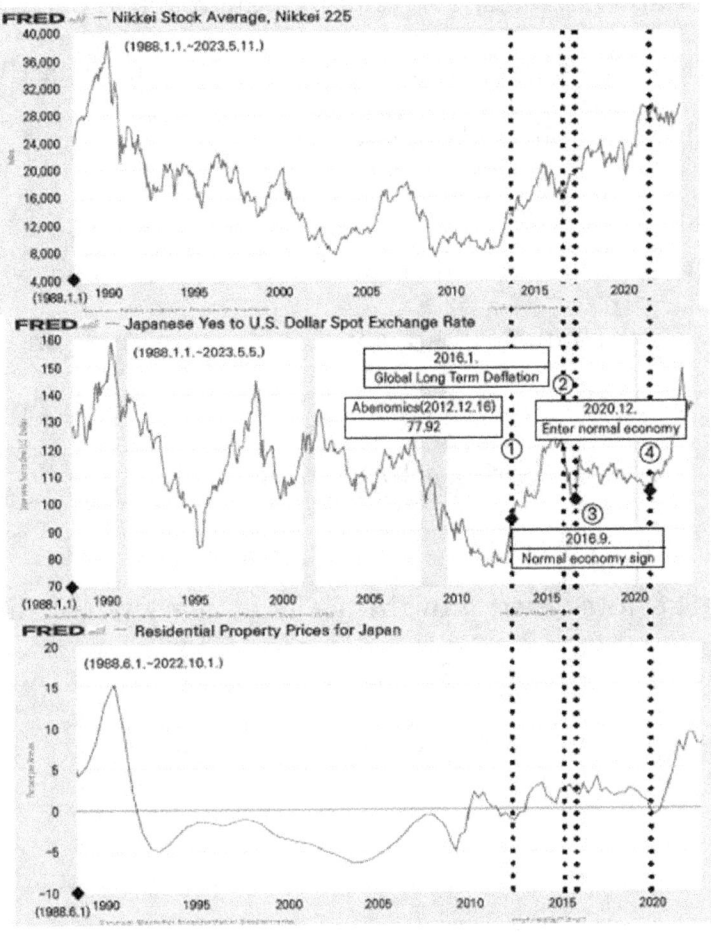

[Fig.18] Changes in the Nikkei, yen exchange rate, and housing index during the 11yrs (2009-2019) Long-Term Deflation

In March 2022, FRED began raising the benchmark

interest rate from 0-0.25% to 5-5.25%, a sharp increase of about 2500%. The inflation rate reached 6.9%.

"Money Poured In, But Europe's 'D' Fears" (Ha Hyun-ok, 'Joongang Ilbo', September 3, 2020)

In an article titled "Prof. Roubini 'US, China will press Asian countries on whose side they are on'" (Kwon Young-mi, 'news1', May 23, 2020), it was claimed that "Corona will bring a 10-year recession".

The forecasted growth rate is at the level of the Great Depression of 1929. However, the world, including the United States, is in a war against inflation.

Of course, raising interest rates could hasten the onset of long term deflation by contracting the economy, but the world is not facing long term deflation solely because of the coronavirus. It is a coincidence that the two phenomena have overlapped.

The world was already in this position before the pandemic. It's completely different from the theory of short term deflation, i.e. a normal recession.

These phenomena cannot be explained or solved by conventional economic theories. That's why Japan's long term deflation, which lasted more than 30 years, was solved in 32 years.

Harry Dent's argument in ⟨The Population Cliff 2018⟩ that the demographic cliff alone will lead to a global deflation is overstated.

The demographic cliff is certainly deflationary because of the decline in consumption, but it is not the sole cause of Japan's 32 years of long term deflation.

The biggest cause of Japan's long term deflation has

been the continued strength of the yen, which has indiscriminately depressed all industries and all products in Japan.

A strong yen, i.e. a weak dollar, indiscriminately and uniformly lowers the price of everything in Japan. This is what Harry Dent missed. The cost savings from a declining population, i.e. deflation, is only a small part of the story.

Japan is not alone in its debt; as of the end of last year, the world's debt was about 30 trillion won, or 3.65 times the GDP of more than 200 countries around the world. It would take three years and eight months to pay off the entire world's income without spending a dime.

Currently, debt and asset prices are increasing simultaneously, but I believe that the world will soon enter a dreaded long term deflation war with the bursting of bubbles like Japan.

In particular, there are reasons why there is no way for Korea to avoid a Japanese-style long term deflation. Just like Japan's curse of the yen, Korea will have a curse of the won.

First, the strong Korean won is the biggest reason.
Like Japan's strong yen, Korea's strong won is likely to continue to hurt its economy.

Second, it goes without saying that the working age population is declining. However, it should be understood as the number of people who can consume, not the literal number.

Finally, there is the debt problem.
The combined debt of the Korean government, enterprises, and households is about 500 trillion won, or

about 2.8 times the GDP. Household debt is 100.9% of GDP, which is higher than 81.2% in the United States and 78% in major industrialized countries.

As household debt grows, the principal and interest payments have to be made, which also leads to a reduction in consumption.

In Japan, the government debt is a whopping 266%.
Even when the bubble bursts, the debt remains, and this debt will drag the economy back into recession. This leads to debt deflation. This becomes a global phenomenon and plunges the world into recession.

The current level of global debt relative to domestic GDP is higher than it was in the 2008 financial crisis, and this time the shock will be too great. The subprime mortgage system is a bigger problem.

As usual when households and enterprises default, banks and other financial institutions will be hit first. A McKinsey report predicts that banks will lose $2-4 trillion in profits by 2024.

[Figure 18]. As the yen rose, the Nikkei rose, and so did the Japanese housing index. It's almost proportional. It can be seen that the investment technique of investing in stocks and real estate according to the price fluctuation of the yen, which was based on the Diamond Dollar Investment Method, should be completely reversed.

By analyzing Japan in the past, you can predict and verify the price of apartments and stocks in Korea for the next 30 years or so through FRED's ultra-long term graphs.

By analyzing Japan over a long period of 75 years, you

can predict the future price of Korean apartment stocks by applying it to Korea.

These points from Japan show that investing in Korea during the curse of the Korean won will be successful if you take them into account. The only way to survive and make a good return on your investment is to completely abandon your traditional thinking.

No one knows that the investment technique in the long term deflation period should be 180 degrees different from the investment technique in the short term deflation period, because the author has analyzed and found it for the first time.

It is worth remembering that [Figure 2] and [Figure 18] go hand in hand. [Figure 2 provides a very long term comparison of the triangular relationship between the Japanese yen-dollar, the Nikkei, and the Japanese housing index over 48 years.

[Figure 18] is a graph that analyzes the triangular relationship between the Japanese yen-dollar, the Nikkei index, and the Japanese housing index over an 11-year period.

The reason why we have to split the graph into two graphs [Figure 2] and [Figure 18] is that Japan's housing index has only been compiled and published since 2009, so there is no Japanese housing index to compare the changes in the yen-dollar exchange rate, the Nikkei index, and house prices over 48 years.

One might ask the author
However, a truly developed country is one that is a member of the 3050 Club of Nations, and only then can it be analyzed whether its economic and population policies are working properly, and its population

problems, debt problems, etc. can be compared. I.e. Korea and Japan are the best comparators.

They are the same manufacturing-based countries and are competitors in every way. Often, the general public and some scholars among the intellectuals say that Korea is different from Japan.

Of course we are different in terms of ethnicity, islands and mainland, language, etc. But the economic foundation, i.e. the strong yen and the strong won, the demographic change problem, the debt problem, etc. are similar. We have to be that similar to be able to compare.

It is the long term deflation that will end this great bull market wave, which will reduce the value of property by 80-90% if left in its current form, but could be 10x or more if handled properly.

In Japan, there was nowhere to invest.

Real estate and stocks have collapsed by 80-90% on average and are now recovering to the prices they were 30 years ago under Abenomics.

Bank deposits in Japan are currently paying around 0% interest. Interest on loans is also around 0%. Interest rates on government bonds are negative and there are no government bonds for sale. Soon, Korea will run out of places to invest, just like Japan did.

The first year of zero interest rates (loan and deposit) in Korea is likely to be around 2026. Zero interest rates mean that you can borrow money from banks at zero interest and invest in rental properties, but you should know in advance that this is a path to death, just like Japan did for 30 years.

It is too similar, as we saw in Japan and South Korea, where the long term deflation lasted for 32 years. So South Korea cannot avoid a Japanese-style long term deflation.

On the other hand, if you prepare in advance, this great crisis is the last chance to transform yourself from a worker to a capitalist. Workers armed with the knowledge of long term deflation from this book should take full advantage of this opportunity. All stocks, apartments gold silver bitcoin, etc. will collapse by 80-90% on average.

I.e., if you look at the United States in the past and Japan until recently, and study and prepare for investment during long term deflation in advance, you will have the opportunity to rise in status, transforming from a salaryman and a poor person into a worker to a capitalist.

On the other hand, it should be remembered that for those who are not prepared with fintech knowledge, long term deflation is not an opportunity, but the "D" of fear.

(Part Two)

Long Term Deflation Is a Complete Jackpot opportunity

The wealth of those who do not invest for the long term deflation that began in January 2016 will naturally and unwittingly transfer to those who have prepared. In a democratic country, wealth is transferred from one citizen to another by war, financial crisis, political crisis, inflation, or deflation.

Only hyperinflation transfers wealth from the private sector to the governments. For the rest of the economic fluctuations, the government has little interest in who gets the wealth.

The wealth of the country as a whole, i.e. the national wealth, is always the same, too. It's during long term deflation and hyperinflation that we see sharp and true wealth transfers, as opposed to the more modest wealth transfers of inflation and short term deflation.

In long term deflation, the value of property such as stocks and apartments collapse by 80-90% in a short period of time. On the other hand, there are also properties that surge by 80-90% compared to those that collapse.

Therefore, if you invest by taking advantage of this opportunity, i.e., in a long term deflation, a large transfer of wealth occurs as quickly as war through short selling, etc. There will be a great transfer of wealth between enterprises and between classes of people, and a new conglomerate can be created.

During a long term deflation, a combination of long term deflationary knowledge and short selling can lead to a change of ownership in an instant. Long term deflation can also be a great opportunity for management wars between enterprises.

After the long term deflation ends, when inflation returns for the next 70 years or so, the difference between getting rich and getting poor will be determined during this period, i.e. during the long term deflation.

In a long term deflationary period, if you leave your wealth in real estate, gold, oil, stocks, etc. as it was in the past, over a period of 10-20 years, i.e. in the long term, they will be destroyed.

The difference between a joyful long term deflation for some and a dreadful long term deflation for others is the difference between studying and preparing in advance and facing a long term deflation year without any measures.

The more developed a country becomes, i.e., the more static the society, the less wealth is transferred between classes. In other words, poverty and wealth are usually inherited in the same way.

In a way, the lottery is the only hope. However, there is an even greater opportunity for wealth transfer than the lottery. In long term deflation, when the price of all real assets drops rapidly over a decade or more, the wealth of those who hold cash and cash equivalents grows not just in absolute value, but also relatively quickly, thanks to interest.

In other words, during deflation, wealth spontaneously shifts from holders of real assets (real estate, stocks, gold, etc.) to holders of cash assets.

The opposite happens during inflation, which is what we've been seeing with the land myth and the continued rise in real estate prices.

In the case of long term deflation, we have the example of Japan, where real assets fell by about 80-90% relative to cash during the lost 30 years. It collapsed to about one-fifth of its value.

Let's go back to the United States during the Great Depression of 1929 for a moment. In Chapter 2, we see that relative values changed by 87.1%. This is all wealth transfer due to changes in relative value. This shows that it's wise to move your wealth into cash and cash equivalents before the downfall.

Therefore, if you know in advance that a long term

deflation, a deflation that lasts for more than five years, is coming and invest in deflation-beating investments, you can increase your wealth by 4 to 10 times and see your wealth skyrocket over the years, compared to those who did not.

In a nutshell, in a long term deflation, you should invest according to the Inverse Diamond Dollar Investment Method and the Pentagon Investment Method.

In Korea & world, the downfall of wealth has already begun. It is important to realize that the fluctuation of property prices is caused by the fluctuation of commodity prices, but mainly by the fluctuation of the dollar price.

Those who use the so-called short term and long term deflation theory in combination with the short selling strategy will be the biggest beneficiaries of the long term deflation war.

I.e., it is during long term deflation that new conglomerates can be created! In a long term deflation war, a new tycoon can be born...

The German ThyssenKrupp conglomerate, the Benz family, and the BMW family were born during hyperinflation. During Japan's long term deflation period, Sony was also shaken up. Toyota's one-year foreign currency loss was 13 trillion yen. In long term deflation and hyperinflation, the ranks of conglomerates change or are created anew.

To make big money shorting stocks, you need to be able to take advantage of the fact that long term deflation usually lasts for more than 20 years and the stock price drops by 90%.Short the stock, but keep shorting it for the whole long term deflation period, i.e. for 20 years, and do not redeem it halfway through.

Your fortune will skyrocket by 90%, and the enterprise you want to buy or someone else's fortune will collapse by 90%, and you will have enough wealth to become a conglomerate. It's a chance for a salaryman to become a capitalist.

Chapter 12)

Investing in a Long Term Deflation

Deflation means an economic recession, and recessions, no matter how long they are, usually end within five years, so we call them short term deflation.

A recession that lasts longer than five years is called a long term deflation. It may not be correct to categorize the economic situation as short term or long term deflation simply by the five-year period.

In normal times, i.e. in booms and busts, the dollar price, stock indices, and apartment prices always move in opposite directions according to the Diamond Dollar Investment Method.

If the normal deflationary period is longer than 5 years, or if the exchange rate and stock index suddenly start to move in the same direction, it should be judged immediately.

The easiest way to determine a country's long term deflation is to look at the daily movement of the stock index and the dollar. It is a normal pattern of stock market behavior that the dollar collapses when the stock market surges, and this is normal behavior. This is the normal relationship between stock prices and the dollar that we have always seen. This is where the Diamond Dollar Investment Method comes into play. The long term deflation around the world is determined by the proportional and inverse relationship between the international price of the dollar, i.e. the dollar index price and the international gold price.

During short term deflation, you should always follow

the Diamond Dollar Investment Method. In short term deflation, i.e. during a normal economy or recession, all assets have an inverse relationship with the dollar.

In other words, as the dollar goes up, the price of stocks and apartments in the country goes down. The relationship between the dollar and stocks, apartments, gold, oil, etc. is always inversely proportional.

But at some point, this inverse relationship starts to turn into a proportional relationship, which is the beginning of long term deflation. You have to watch carefully. This is the easiest way to determine if we are entering a long term deflation. In conclusion, in all cases, short term deflation is progressing and at some point it will turn into long term deflation.

The methodology for determining whether long term deflation has arrived in a country or the world as a whole is different, as discussed in detail in Chapter 9~10.

Since the phenomenon is completely different during short term deflation, i.e. during a normal business cycle, than during long term deflation, the investment approach should be completely different.

First of all, if you look at the investment strategy during a short term deflation, you can invest as you normally would, as the Diamond Dollar Investment Method still applies during this period.

The moment the bubble bursts or a financial crisis occurs, you can sell stocks and enter into a swap transaction, i.e., a swap to the dollar, according to the Pentagon investing method.

Investing according to the Pentagon investing method,

which is based on the Diamond dollar investment method advocated by the author, can multiply your wealth by 2 to 8 times in a short period of time, and you can buy and sell while predicting the entire future of the price of your property.

In [Figure 19], you can see that the price of crude oil and the price of the dollar move in opposite directions. In [Figure 19], the top figure is the international price of the dollar and the bottom figure is the international price of crude oil. This is what we call the Diamond Dollar Investment Method.

In the graph provided by FRED, the dollar international price is a percentage graph with January 2006 as 100%, which is much more convenient to see the relationship between the dollar and crude oil.

The vertical dotted lines through the two figures are the

dollar price and the price of crude oil in the same year. You can see that when the exchange rate increases, the price of crude oil decreases.

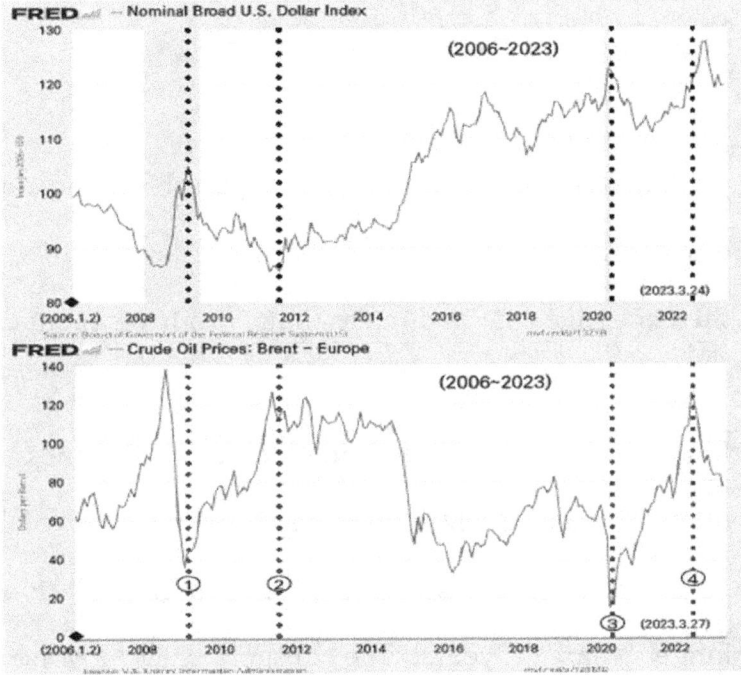

[Fig 19] Inverse relationship between the dollar index and crude oil price from 2016.1.2. to 2021.2.28 (6 years)

When the dollar depreciates, the price of crude oil surges. This is the reason why the Diamond Dollar Investment Method was created.

With this graph, if you can predict the domestic price of the dollar in your country, you can predict the future price of your own property. The six countries that are included in the Dollar Index are easy to predict.

Ordinary investors should not worry about the day-to-day exchange rate, but should take a long term view of the exchange rate and make their own investments.

It has already been explained that one business cycle usually takes 10 years and consists of 5 years of boom and 5 years of recession, i.e. deflation.If deflation lasts longer than 5 years, the author calls it long term deflation.

However, after categorizing deflation into short term deflation and long term deflation according to this criterion, it must be further confirmed by the Diamond

Dollar Investment Method, with the exchange rate and stock index for individual countries and the relationship between the international gold price and the dollar index for international long term deflation.

Therefore, it is important to note that investment products and investment vehicles are completely different in individual countries and internationally.

It is a fact of life that no scholar or economic research institute has seriously studied long term deflation worldwide. This phenomenon, in which the dollar and property prices move according to the inverse Diamond Dollar Investment Method, is the most representative long term deflationary phenomenon that the author first identified.

The vertical dotted line ④ in [Figure 13] and after (A) in [Figure 16] show that the world has already entered a long term deflation in 2016. The vertical dotted line in January 2016 in [Figure 14] also confirms this. However, it is not yet in full swing. It is true that we have already entered long term deflation, as in January 2016.

However, even then, as now, 'if the Diamond Dollar Investment Method is maintained even weakly, long term deflation is not yet in full swing'.

This is because long term deflation and short term deflation are completely different in terms of how to invest and how to escape from it, so you need to look at them in detail, i.e. you should never mistake long term deflation for short term deflation and make reverse investments based on the sequence of rotation between asset markets.

If you believe that long term deflation is in full swing, you should immediately sell stocks and real estate, such as apartments, and buy dollars. Then, when the dollar peaks, it's time to sell and hold cash for a period of time. After that, you should hold government bonds, which are better than cash.

In fact, it is not easy to recognize the moment when we move from short term deflation to long term deflation. [Figure 2] is a graph showing the evolution of the yen price, the Nikkei index, and the housing index over 48 years. The vertical dotted line of BC'② is the short term deflation, i.e., the normal economic state, from the 1970s to December 1988.

After that, i.e. from December 1988, the yen-dollar exchange rate and the Nikkei index suddenly moved in the same direction, i.e. in direct proportion, and Japan's long term deflation began.

Determining this is not easy. However, if the direction of

change of the dollar price and the direction of change of the stock index are the same for six or seven days out of about 10 trading periods, it seems to be the beginning of long term deflation in an individual country.

If we look at the "lost 30 years" of Japan, which was almost the first country in the world to experience long term deflation, except for the United States in the 1930s, the yen-dollar exchange rate surged and the Nikkei index surged from December 1988. Then, from January 1990, stocks fell, apartments fell, and the dollar fell.

1) Within individual countries, you should not buy stocks and apartments simply because they have fallen quite a bit during the short term deflation period. No one knows how long the long term deflation period will last and how much further it will fall.

2) Internationally, with long term deflation in full swing,

you should never buy the dollar and gold you've been wanting to buy just because they're cheap, because there's no telling how much further they'll go down in the long term deflation period, or when they'll go down. If long term deflation continues, the dollar and gold will continue to fall.

This is how to invest in long term deflation. It's actually inaction.

Just hold cash or government bonds while waiting for the long term deflation to end. Readers should always remember that we have said many times that all wealth collapses in a long term deflation.

In a long term deflation, there is no wealth that goes up. In a long term deflation period, deposit rates, lending rates, and even negative interest rates go down to zero, i.e. everything goes down, so there is nowhere to invest anymore, both domestically and internationally.

So Japanese people turn to overseas investments, and even if they make a small profit on their overseas investments due to price appreciation, when they try to bring them back to Japan due to the continuous strengthening of the yen, they realize that they have lost a lot of money when converted to yen.

Since the world entered long term deflation in January 2016, this is what happens when anyone in any country invests overseas. This is the ghost dollar.

The most successful investment strategy in deflation times is to distinguish between short term deflation and long term deflation and invest in the opposite.

In 1988, the Japanese domestic dollar surged 30% in one year, and the Nikkei soared 29% during the same period. Then, on January 1, 1990, the dollar plunged and the

Nikkei began to plummet with the bursting of the bubble. In other words, in Japan, long term deflation began with the surge in the dollar and stock prices.

When long term deflation is in full swing globally, the dollar is no longer cash in individual countries, unless you are a U.S. resident. If you are not a U.S. resident, in a long term deflation country, the dollar is no longer cash, but an investment asset and should be invested, i.e. not owned.

In other words, unless you are a U.S. resident, the dollar will collapse during a long term deflation period because it becomes property, not cash. You can see how serious this would be by looking at the collapse of the dollar in Japan.

Check out the price of the dollar in Japan in December 1988 and the price of the dollar in Japan today, even if only schematically! How much has it collapsed? In the end, we should always remember that in a long term deflation period, everyone should hold their own cash and cash equivalents.

In a long term deflationary period, wealth transfers occur at an accelerated rate, and there is naturally more social disruption. The price of everything in a country that doesn't use the dollar as its everyday currency, i.e., real estate, stocks, etc. is determined by the dollar price, i.e., the exchange rate.

It depends on whether the country is in a normal or long term deflation state. The dollar has an international price and a domestic price. The international price of the dollar is the dollar index price. The dollar index is the average value of six currencies against the US dollar.

The six currencies are: euro 57.6%, yen 13.6%, pound

sterling 11.9%, Canadian dollar 9.1%, krona (Swedish) 4.2%, and franc (Swiss) 3.6%.

Since the dollar exchange rate varies from country to country, it is more accurate to use the Dollar Index to determine whether the dollar has appreciated or depreciated in absolute terms. The Dollar Index price is calculated by the FRB using March 1973 as the base point (100). Published by the FRB.

Therefore, there is no direct relationship between the international price of the dollar and the domestic price, and since the weight of the Japanese yen is 13.6%, the yen price does not have much relationship with the international dollar price.

The euro is the most influential currency as it accounts for more than half of the total. The Korean won is not even included in the six currencies, so it can be said that it has no relationship with the dollar index at all.

[Figure 20] and [Figure 21] show the international price of the dollar and the domestic price of the Korean won. Although it is not easy to predict the exchange rate, we can see that the international price of the dollar has been declining almost continuously if we look at the dollar index graph as a basis for judging future trend changes. We predict that the dollar will continue to trend downward.

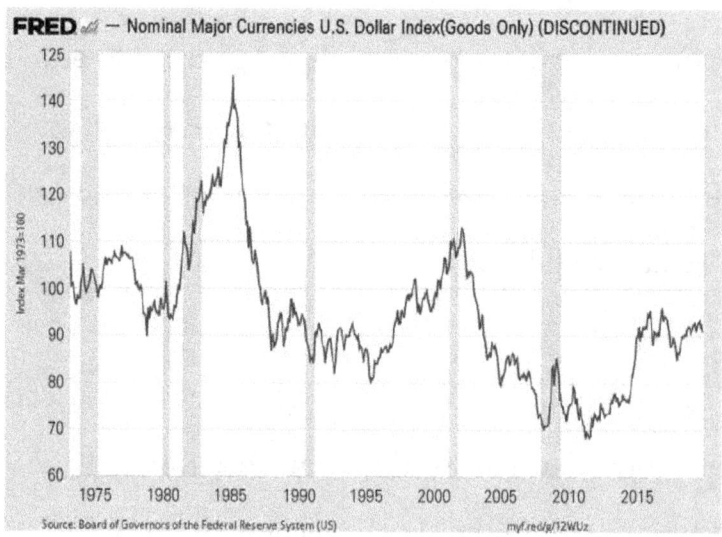

[Fig.20]International Price of the Dollar: Dollar Index (1973.1-

2019.12)

It is the author's experience that when the dollar exchange rate fluctuates significantly, on the scale of 1.5% per day, it can be used as an transition point in the direction of the trend.

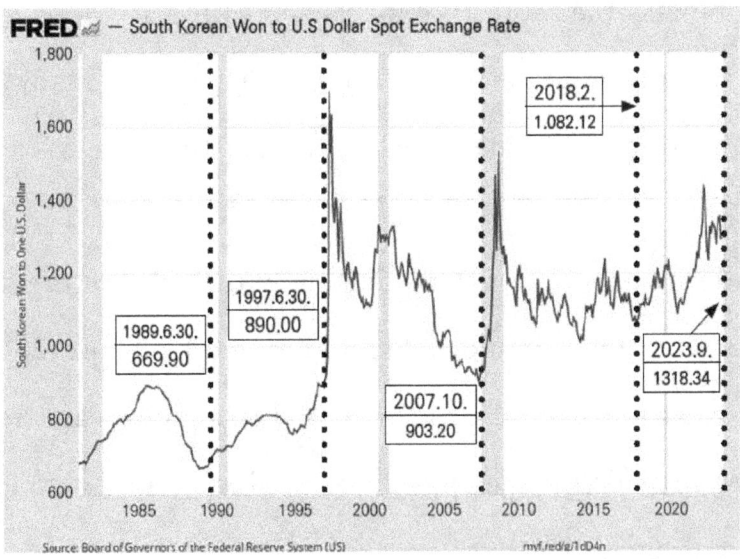

[Fig.21] Prices in South Korea in US Dollars (1981.4 ~2021.4)

As explained earlier, during long term deflation, the dollar price of a party collapses. Why this happens is a matter for economists to study.

In any case, if you look at Japan, which has been in a long term deflation for more than 30 years, you can see the collapse of the exchange rate.

Since Korea is also a long term deflation country like Japan, the author expects the Korean Won to rise sharply and the dollar to fall. There are many other articles predicting a decline in the dollar.

Many experts predict a decline in the price of the dollar. If you look at the dollar index graph [Figure 20], it is clear that the dollar is on a long term downward trend. A falling dollar means that the value of other countries' currencies is rising.

However, there are few experts on Wall Street who disagree that the dollar will fall further. However, no asset is more important than the dollar.

The question is, how much and for how long will it fall? However, there will not be a country to rival the United States in 100 years. China wouldn't last a few months in the economic and financial chaos that would ensue if trade with the United States were cut off.

The United States produces a quarter of the world's wealth, has a population of nearly 400 million, and dominates the Pacific and Atlantic oceans. The U.S. also has military forces in more than 150 countries. The dollar is almost the only international currency.

The U.S. dollar is cash inside the United States, but it is one of the most important forms of property outside the United States. Outside the U.S., the dollar is cash in normal times, but in a crisis, it suddenly becomes more property.

Almost all international transactions are conducted in dollars, i.e., US dollars are everything. Knowing the dollar is the key to success, whether it's in finance or running a country.

One place where the dollar truly is everything is Argentina.

When Argentines buy and sell real estate in their country, they do so only in dollars, not in their currency, the peso.

They do this simply because fluctuations in the exchange rate have a greater impact on the price of real estate, so they now only trade in dollars to ensure that the price of real estate reflects only the price changes caused by pure supply and demand. The Argentines have gotten smart.

Fellow South American country Venezuela has started to

trade all of its goods exclusively in dollars. The same principle of excluding dollar fluctuations from real estate transactions in Argentina also applies to real estate transactions in Venezuela, which recently announced that it will accept Bitcoin as its currency. They're torn.

Countries with extreme dollar fluctuations have simply begun to ignore the fluctuations in the price of their properties as the dollar goes up and down and simply trade goods based on supply and demand.

The public is smart.
They are right.
They've learned from experience, not from the government.
In a long term deflation, it is especially easy to make contrarian investments.

The fact that under normal conditions, i.e., short term deflation and inflation, everything that has a property value is priced in the opposite direction of the dollar should not be applied to long term deflation.

In a short term deflation, the author argues that all investments should be invested against the direction of the dollar. Stocks, apartments, dollars, government bonds, everything. The same goes for gold, silver, and crude oil.

However, in a long term deflation, the investment methodology is reversed again. In a long term deflation, you need to invest in the same direction as the dollar to survive.

This is something that even economists don't quite understand.

It's the golden rule.

This is the conclusion drawn by tracking the relationship between the dollar and other assets for about 40 years after 1990 in Japan.

You should always keep in mind that the fluctuations in the price of the domestic dollar will cause huge changes in the value of your investments. Changes in the price of the dollar, i.e. changes in the exchange rate, also transfer wealth from me to others.

When the dollar goes up, all the stocks, apartments, gold, oil, etc. in the world go down proportionally, and when the dollar goes down, all the stocks, apartments, gold, oil, etc. in the world go up proportionally.

Here's a simple explanation.
Let's say an American wants to buy shares of Samsung Electronics. Let's pretend that the price of a stock doesn't change.

One share of Samsung Electronics costs 59,000 won... at an exchange rate of 1,100 won... Foreigners, including Americans, can buy one share for 53.6$.

One share of Samsung Electronics at 59,000 won... Exchange rate 800 won... Foreigners, including Americans, can buy one share for $73.75.

If the exchange rate goes down, foreigners, including Americans, will have to pay $73.75 - $53.60 = $20.15 more to buy the same Samsung Electronics stock because the domestic price of the dollar has gone down.

Since we have assumed that the price of Samsung Electronics does not actually increase or decrease in Korea due to exchange rate fluctuations, when the exchange rate actually decreases, i.e. when the domestic price of the dollar is cheaper, foreigners will have to pay

20.15$ more for one share of Samsung Electronics.

If the exchange rate decreases, the price of Samsung Electronics stock in Korea will have to increase by $20.15 to get the right price. Therefore, the price of Samsung Electronics in Korea will increase by 1100/800 ×100%=37.5%.

Why would a foreigner pay 37.5% more for Samsung Electronics when the enterprise hasn't changed at all, just because of a sharp drop in the exchange rate? In the end, a stronger won increases the value of Korean assets and provides foreign investors with exchange gains.

If the stronger won is a trend, foreigners will not be able to resist buying Korean stocks because of the lure of the exchange rate. This is evidenced by the rush of dollar funds into the Japanese asset market after the Plaza Accord in 1985.

It is often said that a stronger won is negative for exports because it weakens international competitiveness, but Korea is not the same country anymore. It is actually the number one country in international competitiveness in manufacturing. In terms of quality competitiveness, it is one or two in the world.

Therefore, there is no reason to worry about a sharp rise in the exchange rate, and the quality competitiveness has made it possible to pass on the price decrease in the exchange rate. It is obvious that the dollar has an advantage in inflation or hyperinflation, but not in long term deflation.

In a long term deflation, the domestic dollar collapses like in Japan. We explained earlier that Korea has already experienced long term deflation in 2016. This is the biggest cause of the Korean won's strength.

The strength of this is evident in the long term graph of the yen-dollar exchange rate in Figure 7, which shows the price trend of the Japanese yen against the domestic dollar in Japan. The dollar in countries with long term deflation, i.e., in individual countries around the world, is destined for a major collapse.

The main economic phenomenon of long term deflation is the collapse of the domestic dollar in the country of origin, i.e. in individual countries, and the corresponding collapse of stock prices and apartment prices. Internationally, a collapse of the international gold price awaits to match the collapse of the dollar index.

Chapter 13)
Best: Only Invest in Gov.Bonds During Step 5

In 2024, in the author's new book 'Dollar Swap Fintech make 800% (Assets Market Rotation Investing Formula) Pentagon Investing Method.Subtitle:Tears of Japan', I argued, with evidence, that the world has already been in a long term deflation state since January 2016.

Whether it's a short term deflation or a long term deflation, the last asset in the Pentagon investing method's five-step investment assets should be gov. bonds. That's because gov. bonds are the only one of the five assets that generate income.

Since recession is at its peak, when interest rates are at their lowest level, this is the order in which you should invest in gov. bonds, the last asset in the Pentagon investing method.

Even in a long term deflation, the last five steps of the Pentagon investing method should be gov. bonds.A long term deflation is a long period of recession in which interest rates must continue to fall for at least 5 to 30 years, as they did in the U.S. during the Great Depression and Japan in the 1990s. Interest rates have been falling or at their lowest for 22 years in the US and 32 years in Japan.

Since interest rates and gov. bond prices are always inversely related, you should always invest in gov. bonds in the last five stages of the asset market cycle, and the difference between the duration and duration of the interest rate decline is the difference between a normal business cycle, i.e. short term deflation or long term deflation.

This has left a significant gap in the yields of gov. bonds. Japan has had the world's longest continuous period of negative interest rates due to 32 years of long term deflation. Until March 2024, the interest rate was -0.1%. After 8 years of negative interest rates, Japan exited negative interest rates by raising rates to 0~0.1%.

Now that Japan is exiting long term deflation, it will continue to raise interest rates and normalize them to reach the Plaza Accord level.

As a result, Japan's net foreign investment financial

assets of about $3.5 trillion will begin to move, sending global financial markets into a turbulent state. At the time of the Plaza Accord, the Japanese yen was 240 yen to dollar, and the lowest yen price during the long term deflation was 76.34 yen.

Now, interest rates are slowly returning to normalization, or rather, to the old yen exchange rate. Whenever Japan raises interest rates, the world's financial markets have always been tumultuous.

Looking at the Pentagon investing method, which is a spontaneously created asset market investment cycle in the asset market, which was originally researched and published by the author, money has spontaneously (?) created and circulated an asset market cycle, which is the investment order of the five investment target assets, according to human greed, i.e., the greed to always take more profits.

It's just that we, the investors, have only now been able to organize this asset cycle properly for the first time through the author.

Money is always driven by the human desire to make more profit, so the big five assets - stocks, apartments, dollars, savings, and government bonds - must move in a pentagonal pattern, because that's where the biggest returns are.

The starting date for investing in stocks in any country can be determined by looking at the annual balance of payments a year ago. Whether the balance of payments was in deficit or surplus a year ago is used to determine whether a new business cycle has begun. Whether the previous cycle was a normal short term deflation or a long term deflation, the start of a new cycle is determined by the surplus or deficit of the balance of payments.

The impact of the balance of payments on any country is enormous. A change in the balance of payments is the start of a new business cycle. How much a country's economy depends on trade is represented by its trade dependence. South Korea's trade dependency is 70%. There is nothing Korea can't make and nothing it doesn't make.

That's why the world's media and economists always pay attention to the previous month's Korean import and export statistics released at the beginning of every month. By looking at Korea, we can easily predict the upcoming global economy.

.

In case of South Korea

1) As soon as the annual balance of payments becomes positive a year ago, you should start investing in stocks.

2) After buying stocks, you should invest in apartments because apartments start to rise six months later.

3) Stocks and apartments will continue to rise for 3-4 years, with the leading stocks rising 4-20 times, and then you should sell both stocks and apartments at the right time and do a dollar swap, because in a short period of time, stocks and apartments will collapse and the dollar will soar. The apartment will increase by the same degree as the stock.

4) Next, you need to sell the dollar, which has risen sharply in a short period of time and then started to fall sharply. By now, the government has already raised the standard rate several times to cool down the overheated economy.

Investors who sell their dollars and put them into a term deposit with a significantly higher interest rate will have entered the fourth and most profitable stage of the investment process.

5) About a year after standard interest rates start to rise, they stop to raise them any further and look at the plateau to judge the effectiveness of a rate hike. After that, when they think the economy has calmed down, they will start to lower the standard interest rate once or twice from the plateau. Now, all you have to do is buy Treasury bonds and enjoy.

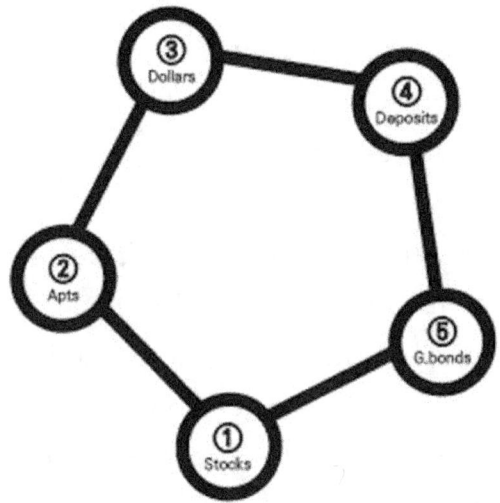

Since you're only investing in gov.bonds, the interest is always paid on time, and the standard interest rate is constantly falling, so your capital gains will continue to grow.

The balance of payments has been in deficit for years. Governments have long since started lowering standard interest rates to stimulate the economy. Once the standard interest rates are lowered and the balance of payments is back in the black, readers can start investing in stocks again.

This is the formula for the Pentagon investing method.

Pentagon investing method is always based on these five steps. This sequence is always the same, so there can be no new investment theories, because this is all there is. This is all there is to it.

In a short term deflation period, i.e. a normal business cycle, the investment period for gov. bonds is only about 2-3 years, but in a long term deflation period, the investment period for gov. bonds is a long time, until 2029 in Korea and 2043 in the world. Until then, you can only invest in gov. bonds and enjoy capital gains and interest.

In Japan's case, they had to invest in only gov. bond for 32 years.

As the standard interest rate kept falling, even to negative interest rates, the capital gains kept growing, and the interest on gov. bonds kept increasing, so the yield was the best among many assets. There's nothing left to invest in.

Whether short term deflation or long term deflation is over or not, of course, should be judged by the surplus or deficit of the balance of payments a year ago. The dollar exchange rate of an individual country and the domestic stock index of that country have changed in a proportional relationship or not is the standard for judgment.

Secondly, another standard rate is whether the Diamond Dollar Investment Method is working properly.

Also, the end of long term deflation can be confirmed by whether the dollar index and international gold prices have begun to move in opposite directions. These are the same rules of investing in any country, forever.

By doing this, you will automatically know when to buy stocks, apartments, dollars, deposits, and government bonds and when to sell them, and if you know these times, you actually know how to make money.
This is the Pentagon investing method, the asset market investment cycle.

Samsung, a famous South Korean electronics enterprise, has more than $136 trillion in cash (as of September 2022), collected from the sale of its founder's soulful office building long ago. Hyundai Motor Group also has 61 trillion won in cash on hand.

A "prominent investor" in the U.S. has accumulated 223 trillion won as of the end of 2023. Apple also has billions of dollars in 0.25% corporate bonds. Apple issues corporate bonds when interest rates are low in the U.S., and stocks up huge amounts of money for a long term, paying interest.
This is true fintech, i.e. financial management techniques.

By the end of 2023, the big South Korean investors had accumulated 618 trillion won, earning almost no interest. In 2024, of course, it will be in time deposits with higher interest rates. That's how fast the big investors are.

A thorough analysis of Japan's lost 32 years concludes that cash is king, and it seems that South Korea's conglomerates, Samsung, Hyundai, and other big investors have realized this and prepared for it. Analyzing Japan's lost 30 years shows that in a long term deflation, there is nowhere to invest.

In 32 years (1989-2020), Japan collapsed by as much as 90% in all prices, including the dollar price of stocks and apartments. In January 2016, the world experienced a long term deflation, so eventually the world, including Korea, will have nowhere to invest, just like Japan 32 years ago.

In a long term deflation, if you invest or respond like a short term deflation or a normal recession, you are completely ruined. It's completely backward-looking.

This book is the world's first and only full-scale study of long term deflation. I believe that the research on Japan's collapse by some economics professors, research institutes, etc. is insufficient compared to this book.

Moreover, if you rely on sensationalized information from YouTube, you will be ruined by the conflict of fragmented knowledge. To gain financial knowledge, you need to read books and organize comprehensive theories on your own, not what YouTubers say.

For 32 years, real-world evidence from Japan has shown that investing in anything is a recipe for failure.

Starting in 2023, a "famous investor" in the U.S. invested in Japanese stocks and issued yen-denominated bonds locally and had the Bank of Japan underwrite the bonds. This is equivalent to borrowing yen locally.

With this money, he has been investing in the five largest Japanese trading companies. Why would he borrow in yen if he didn't have dollars?

The reason is that he knows that the yen will strengthen further and further in the future, and he knows that when the yen strengthens again someday, he plans to return with the profits of his investment at a favorable exchange rate. He is not borrowing Japanese yen locally because he has no dollar funds.

Why gov.bonds are best in a long term deflation environment

When long term deflation strikes

Like the U.S. in the 1930s or Japan in 1989, stocks, apartments, dollars, gold, whatever you invest in collapse by 90% or less. Cash or short term gov. bonds are almost in place, but other assets collapse, so the price of the asset increases relatively. This is called an opportunity profit.

Therefore, cash and cash equivalents, such as cash and long term gov. bonds, are the best investments during long term deflation. During a long term deflation period, the standard interest rate is constantly falling, so long term gov. bonds will skyrocket.

During short term deflation,

The dollar, stocks, apartments, gold, crude oil, etc. move in opposite directions, but in long term deflation, they all move in the same direction. This is a phenomenon that no one quite understands.

No economics professor or research institute understands this, which is why Japan has been struggling with long term deflation for 32 years. Therefore, investors should also know how to invest in gov. bonds correctly.

You should also know that gov. bonds can collapse by more than 90% if you choose the wrong time to invest.

In addition, bonds are an investment asset that should be invested in the last investment stage of the asset market, stage 5, according to the Pentagon investing method, which is a cyclical investment method in the asset market. This technique of investing in bonds should be completely different from what we are used to.

When it's normal times

In normal times, there is no reason to invest in any bonds, even gov. bonds that pay pennies on the bonds. In addition, at the end of a recession, all bonds, except for gov. bonds, are exposed to the risk of interest suspension or default, so there is no reason to invest in bonds in normal times, except for market gains.

Moreover, high yield bonds are not something you'd want to hold for the rest of your life. The same goes for corporate and municipal bonds. If a gov. bond has a maturity of one or two years, or even a long term government bond, it is the same as a short term government bond, and you can treat it like cash.

For 32 years in Japan, investing in anything was a shortcut to ruin, and now we're seeing the same long term deflation phenomenon in Korea and everywhere else in the world. This is long term deflation.

There are only a few assets that can actually make money, such as the KODEX 2002x inverse, a product that doubles the standard interest rate when the US interest rate goes up, and a product that always pays a dividend of 6% or more, even in the face of inflation or deflation.

In a long term deflation period, cash is king. Not gold, bitcoin, etc. You need to have cash and cash equivalents. That's why South Korea has Samsung, Hyundai, and other companies that have cash in reserve.

In a long term deflation period, everything, i.e. all the goods in the world, collapse in price. This time, the deflation that hit the world is not just a short term deflation, i.e., a recession that will return to its original price after a year or two, but a long term deflation that will last at least three years and up to 30 years.

Therefore, the importance of cash cannot be overemphasized. The scope of cash includes bank deposits and cash equivalents such as short term gov. bonds and matured government bonds...

Another thing to keep in mind is the dollar. The dollar is a monster.

The dollar is always cash for people in the United States. Outside the United States, the dollar is also cash during normal times. However, when a country faces a foreign exchange crisis or economic crisis, the dollar becomes more of a property and is no longer simply cash.

In other words, in short term deflation, the dollar will soar, and in long term deflation, the dollar will collapse like other commodities.So, outside of the United States, the dollar has three different characteristics: cash, soaring asset, and falling asset. The dollar is not just cash, it's a monster asset because it can be a great asset and then it can be cash and then it can be a monster asset.

Another thing

Cash and deposits do not change in price to the extent that their value can be said to change, so they cannot be considered as an investment asset in normal times, but there is another reason why they become the best investment asset in a crisis such as long term deflation.

Cash is one of the best investments assets because the relative value of cash increases indefinitely in line with the collapse of real assets.

If all goods of property value collapse in a long term

deflation, the relative value of cash and cash equivalents will increase by the same amount as the collapse. Opportunity profits are generated, making it one of the best investments.

However, there are better investments asset than cash and cash equivalents.

That is, long term gov. bonds with a maturity of one year or more. In a long term deflation, they become almost the only last effective investment. They are like cash in a time deposit.

However, if you continue to hold long term gov. bonds, the price of gov. bonds will continue to rise because the interest rates in the market will have to be constantly lowered to stimulate the economy during long term deflation. At this time, you should definitely invest in gov. bonds.

You should never invest in bonds other than gov. bonds. This is because it's a time of financial depression and there will be many defaults. However, government bonds guarantee capital gains and interest income for as long as you hold them.

Unless the country goes bankrupt, these bonds are always guaranteed to be paid. After the establishment of the Korean government in 1945, the Ministry of Reconstruction bonds, i.e. the current government bonds, were issued as compulsory government bonds. As a result, they traded for a long time as paper, worthless, believing that the government would never pay them back.

After the government was established and the country's finances became stronger, the bonds were redeemed for cash, as expected. There is also an episode where a construction company called Youngdong Development and Promotion, which bought the Ministry of Reconstruction bonds and stored them in warehouses when it was unclear whether they would be repaid, became a conglomerate cash cow.

As mentioned above, among all types of bonds in the market, the only investment should be government bonds, so we will only talk about investing in government bonds from now on. Gov. bonds are almost the same as cash, as long as they are liquid, so let's take a look at some tips for investing in gov. bonds.

Key tips for investing in gov.bonds that are often misunderstood

1) You should not invest in any bonds other than gov. bonds, whether in normal times or in times of crisis. Even gov. bonds are not a good investment asset in normal times, i.e., you should not invest in any bonds except gov. bonds, let alone in times of crisis.

In normal times, bonds will only earn you a few pennies in interest and no capital gains.

The most fundamental problem is that households, enterprises, governments, etc. always need money in times of danger, i.e. at the beginning of a full blown recession. This is when bond issuance becomes a boom. Because it's a recession.

Therefore, investing in bonds other than gov. bonds at the beginning of a recession is suicidal, because the recession will soon deepen, and everything will be destroyed by unsold apartments, collapsing stocks, defaults, interest payment suspensions, etc. With the exception of government bonds, the higher the interest rate, the riskier the bond, and therefore the more dangerous it is to buy.

The author believes that even gov. bonds should be bought in the second round, after the interest rates start to fall. If you do invest in bonds, always invest only in gov. bonds, but only after you have seen the standard interest rate drop by the second round.

As we saw with the SVB bank failure in the US, even gov. bonds can be a very risky investment if you invest during a period of rising interest rates.

2) Corporate bonds bank bonds municipal bonds etc. should not be invested even in normal times. Not to mention in the beginning of a recession. In good times,

you should invest in high-yielding assets such as stocks or apartments, according to the Pentagon investing method. In good times, you shouldn't be blinded by the few pennies of interest paid on all bonds, including gov. bonds.

3) In conclusion, bonds are the only possible investment asset in a recession, but only if the standard interest rate has been cut once or twice and the future direction of the interest rate is predicted.

For foreigners, investing in U.S. gov. bonds, U.S. stocks, and U.S. real estate, i.e., all overseas investments, is possible only if the exchange rate rises in the long term.

4) You should not invest in gov. bond ETFs because you cannot control the holding period, interest rate, and price of the bond.

5) Gov. bonds are bonds issued by the government, so they are like cash.

They pay interest every quarter unless the country goes bankrupt. The price changes according to the standard interest rate, but at maturity, you get 100% of your principal back. The standard interest rate is usually around 2-3%, and bond prices collapse when interest rates rise and soar when they fall.

In conclusion, you shouldn't invest in bonds other than government bonds, i.e. municipal bonds, corporate bonds, etc. in good times or bad. The market is advising you to invest in gov. bonds in anticipation of a drop in the standard interest rate, which is quite unlikely.

The problem is that this time, the high standard interest rates will last for a long time, more than 2-3 years, so you should realize that it's time to wait it out and stay in time deposits.

6) Changes in interest rates and bond prices

For a 10-year gov. bond, the price of the bond will rise and fall by about 7% as the standard interest rate rises and falls by 1%.

The reason why I use the words "explosion" and "collapse" for this 7% price fluctuation is that it is safe enough to bet all your money, so it is common to invest a large amount of money in gov. bonds, so the total amount of profit is huge, and it is also an asset that rarely fluctuates in price during normal times.

Currently, there are a lot of books on the market about

investing in gov. or corporate bonds, but they are not very helpful. There is very little information to be gained from reading a book.

The fact that if the standard interest rate goes down by 1%, the price of a 10-year bond goes up by 7%. This is a key piece of information for bond investing, and it doesn't tell you that.

The key information is that the 20-year bond will naturally rise 14% when the standard interest rate drops by 1%, and the 30-year bond will immediately jump 21%. The reverse is also true, with a proportional decrease.

This is the actual price at which the bond should be traded on the market, based on the present value (NPV) of the total interest you will receive in the future, so it is slightly lower than the theoretical calculation.

7) Capital gains disappear like smoke at maturity.

You can only capitalize on capital gains if you sell before maturity. The highest gov. bond yield in history was 15.19% per annum during the Paul Volcker years.

8) Perpetual bonds are not an investment at all.

Swiss Credit Suisse's perpetual bonds were cut without any compensation. You can buy and sell Korean perpetual bonds (new capital securities) only after you understand their contents, but in any case, they are not an investment because they are worse than gov. bonds.

Limitations of investing in gov. bonds

While gov. bonds are the best investment in a long term deflation environment, it's important to recognize the limitations of investing in gov. bonds.

First, the market is immature and the difference between the transaction price and the theoretical price is large.

The bond price should change exactly as the interest rate changes. Korea has a small bond issuance volume and weak bond liquidity, i.e., gov. bond market prices are always distorted.

A small number of institutional investors own most of the bonds, so there is a small amount of bonds in circulation, which prevents a fair price from being formed when the standard interest rate changes.

There is a separate market for bonds in the stock market, i.e., the securities market. Bonds such as gov. bonds can be bought and sold through HTS(Home Trading System), a securities company. However, the Korean bond market does not have a large trading volume, so it is not possible to buy and sell at a fair price.

In this case, there are gov. bond ETFs listed on the stock market as a substitute for spot gov. bonds. Therefore, in the case of Korea, where the bond market is not developed, i.e. the volume of bonds in circulation is small and the price is not fair, it is possible to buy and sell through bond ETFs.

Buying and selling through them can have a similar effect to owning actual gov. bonds. There are short term bond ETFs, such as the 3-year gov. bond, the 5-year gov. bond, the 10-year gov. bond, the 20-year gov. bond, and so on.

However, there is a limitation that bond investors cannot adopt a strategy of holding the bonds to maturity, as the distributors of these bond ETF products always replace the underlying gov. bonds to match the maturity of the bonds, such as 2-10 years. Also, it is not always clear if the full amount of interest is paid out each time.

As long term deflation progresses, standard interest rates are bound to fall steadily as it progresses. In response, gov. bond prices will spike and spike and spike. The author believes that Korea's long term deflation will end in 2029 and the rest of the world's long term deflation will end around 2048.

In a long term deflation, the relative value of cash continues to rise, i.e., it doesn't actually go up, but everything else in the world goes down - real estate, stocks, necessities, gold, silver, etc. That's why cash is the best asset.

I say cash is best even if it doesn't grow in absolute terms, i.e., it earns almost no interest, whereas gov. bonds go up in price every year in addition to the interest they promise.

In the case of Japan, which had a long term deflation for 32 years, the standard interest rate was continuously lowered to a negative rate. The world, including Korea, has been experiencing long term deflation since January 2016. Sooner or later, Korea's standard interest rates will fall to negative rates, just like Japan's.

During a long term deflation period, it is important to continue to hold gov. bonds to earn interest income, and as standard interest rates decline over the long term, the market gains from the decline in interest rates will increase.

It is worth noting that it is better to delay entering the stock market when the balance of payments shows a one-year annual trade surplus than to enter the stock market immediately. It is safer to sell long term government bonds and start investing in stocks after the government has raised the standard interest rate once or twice.

Entering a long term deflation always starts from a short term deflation, so when judging the exit of a long term deflation, it is also judged from the definite end of a short term deflation.

This can be judged from the increase in the standard interest rate, i.e., the exit from long term deflation can also be judged from the start of the increase in the standard interest rate.

However, the judgment of a clear exit from international long term deflation should be judged from the restoration of the proportional relationship between the dollar index price and the international gold price.

Second, the time when everyone, and I mean everyone,

needs money is coincidentally at the end of a recession. When households, enterprises, and governments all really need money, it's almost always at the end of a recession.

However, bonds, including gov. bonds, are not good investments during normal times because they have little price fluctuation and earn only small interest income.

In general, bonds, including gov. bonds, become an investment asset only during a financial crisis, i.e., even the safest gov. bonds should not be invested in normal times, but only during the fifth stage of the Pentagon investing method, i.e., when the recession is at its peak.

This is because when a recession is in full swing, the standard interest rate will soon rise sharply and the price of gov. bonds will skyrocket. As a result, bonds, including gov. bonds, should only be invested in a severe recession.

After all, gov. bonds, municipal bonds, corporate bonds, bank bonds, etc.
because of their low interest rates in normal times,
In times of crisis, you should not invest in any other bonds except gov. bonds to avoid the various risks that occur during a recession.

In the end, I don"t recommend investing in any bonds for the rest of your life except gov. bonds. This author also doesn't invest in municipal bonds.

It is important to note that in the past, municipal bonds have often stopped paying for a significant period of time due to local gov. defaults in the United States.

Never invest in corporate bonds, municipal bonds, etc. and always invest in gov. bonds, but even in gov. bonds, the investment opportunity should only be invested once, at the very end of the business cycle.

Since one business cycle takes 10 years, even if it is gov. bonds, once every 10 years, at the beginning of the cycle, you should invest in gov. bonds, which are the last five investment target assets of the Pentagon investing method, by canceling the time deposit and investing for about 2-3 years. Normally, gov. bonds are never an investment.

However, in the case of a long term deflation depression, there will be a long period of falling interest rates, and in severe cases, negative interest rates for several years, so you should hold on to them, enjoying the interest and capital gains, and then sell them when the standard interest rate increases at least once or twice.

This is the beginning of a new decade of economic turbulence, and this is when you should sell your bonds and start investing in stocks. In conclusion, gov. bonds are the best investment in a long term deflation environment. This is because you can enjoy both interest and capital gains over the long term.

Things to keep in mind

Third, Japan began selling government bonds for individuals in 2003. The South Korean government will issue gov. bonds for personal investment around June 2024. It will be sold only to individuals within a limit of 100 million won per person.

It is a gov. bond that can be repurchased, cannot be sold on the market, and pays interest at maturity with compound interest. They have little liquidity, and the interest is too low.

The government issues gov. bonds with the goal of collecting money from the market. By inflating the current bubble further, the government will be able to collect large sums of money from private investors. Readers should not be fooled by these strange government bonds.

Fourth, long term gov. bonds are not a safe haven asset. This is due to price movements and lack of liquidity when standard interest rates are cut or raised. Even with gov. bonds, you need to be aware of the changing system.

Since the SVB default in the US in 2023, US Treasury Secretary Janet Yellen has taken measures to ensure that US gov. bonds are currently recognized at par value, i.e., regardless of their current value, even if prices collapse.

If U.S. gov. bonds were valued at market value, many banks would be bankrupt. Banks are by far the largest holders of U.S. gov. bonds, and countries hold a large percentage of their foreign reserves in U.S. gov. bonds.

It is also important to note that the collapse in the price of U.S. gov. bonds is not recognized in their foreign exchange reserves, as discussed in [Chapter 6], and South Korea's foreign exchange reserves have also suffered severe valuation losses, reducing their actual holdings.

A recent example is the perpetual corporate bonds issued by Swiss Credit Suisse in the course of UBS's M&A of Credit Suisse, which were destroyed for free. The supposedly safe bank bonds issued by the bank were destroyed for free.

Perpetual bonds, otherwise known as new capital

securities. This is also a monster corporate bond. It is a monster that the issuer can change in its advantage without any compensation.

Currently, there are perpetual bonds issued by Korean steelmaker POSCO, state-owned power company KEPCO, former Doosan Heavy Industries and Construction, and several Korean banks. It is important to check the issuance terms, conversion terms, and burning terms of these bonds. I don't think any investor has read all the terms and conditions.

I think there are big losses waiting for investors here. The recent sale of HMM could not be finalized because of the new capital securities already issued. The world is a minefield if you look closely. Therefore, you should never invest based on popular YouTube videos and fragmented economic knowledge.

Finally, let's take a look at the most important gov bonds bubble trade of all...

1) Readers should be aware that, according to the asset market's cyclical investment sequence, if you buy a gov. bond and realize capital gains due to a decline in interest rates, the capital gains will disappear if you hold it until maturity. Therefore, you should sell when the standard interest rate is at its lowest point, i.e. when the price of govt. bonds is at its highest point.

2) On the other hand, if you buy a gov. bond that has already dropped due to rising interest rates and hold it until maturity, you can enjoy all the gains. In this case, you can enjoy the capital gains, i.e., it is best to buy when the price of the govt. bonds collapses.

Therefore, when a country experiences a financial crisis, foreign exchange crisis, or a general decline in popularity, foreign investors should sell their gov. bonds to avoid currency exchange losses and the collapse of the gov. bond price. This is the best opportunity for long term investment in gov. bonds.

A specific example is the Paul Volcker era of the 1970s. In December 1980, i.e. at the end of the third wave of inflation, the highest yield (standard interest rate) on US gov. bonds was a whopping 22%. In 1981, a long term investment in U.S. gov. bonds would have paid 22% for 30 years. That's unthinkable today.

.In 1974, i.e. during the Paul Volcker era, the inflation rate was (11.0%), and in 2021, the inflation rate is (9.1%). What will be the peak gov yield of this third wave?

Comparing the 22% gov yield in the 1980s with the expected gov yield this time around, calculated using the proportional formula, the expected gov yield is a whopping (11.9%), i.e. the gov yield could reach 11.9% this time around.

The author is holding cash and Macquarie Infrastructure Fund to protect against this.

It's worth remembering that this war against inflation is very similar to the Paul Volcker era.

It is a historical fact that inflation always goes through three waves of rises and falls before it converges to its target. We are now halfway through wave 1, which is why cash is always best in long term deflation.

Chapter 14)

Second Best : Short stocks, Apartments, too

Don't Hold the Dollar in a Long Term Deflation. Take Advantage of thePerfect Short Selling Opportunity! Shorting stocks can make you a lot of money over the long term. You can also make a lot of money shorting stocks

in the short term.

Long-term short selling, especially when combined with the author's theory of long term deflation, is a great opportunity to short all stocks, grains, commodities, gold, etc. with the ability to accurately predict the extent and duration of a long term decline in advance.

Long-term deflation takes a minimum of 22 years and a

maximum of 30 years, as seen in the U.S. in 1929 and Japan in 1990, and apartments, stocks, etc. plummet by up to 80-90% before the period begins, including the previous and subsequent declines.

Based on these two facts, short selling stocks, apartments, gold, etc. is a complete jackpot opportunity that can change your position to become an employer or remain a worker.

You can short the stock directly or buy KODEX 200 Inverse or KODEX Inverse Leverage and make a lot of money safely.

You can also short apartments.

Shorting apartments may sound unfamiliar to you, but you can accurately predict the market price according to the theory of long term deflation, so you can sell your apartment when it is expensive and buy it back at the bottom, which is the same effect as shorting stocks, so remember everything, I am saying that you can short apartments.

The opportunity for wealth to fall and move, and for new wealth to be created, is open to everyone. Long-term deflation is as big a money war as hyperinflation, changing the ranks and fortunes of the tycoons.

As long term deflation progresses, the price of the dollar plummets, international gold prices plummet, stock prices plummet, and apartment prices plummet. For 30 years, there's nothing left to invest in, like in Japan. So it's an economic phenomenon that no one has ever experienced before, and it can last for 22 to 30 years.

If you have a long term deflation for more than 30 years, it means that the price of the dollar and the price of gold in that country have been falling or weakening for more than 30 years.

In other words, conglomerates and exporters should know that when a long term deflation is in full swing, a big money war is just around the corner.

Export conglomerates will see their profits continue to shrink as the dollar continues to depreciate day after day.

Small and mid-sized companies will see a prolonged decline in the price of their imported commodities. Therefore, their profits increase every day, so they are happy.

The Japanese conglomerates that were reaching for the sky before 1989 began to fizzle out due to the long term deflation in Japan, without them even realising it.

Sony has gone from being the world's top electronics company to having a hard time staying afloat. TOYOTA's foreign currency translation losses alone amounted to 13 trillion yen in sales for the year.

This shows that these Japanese conglomerates had not been able to cope with long term deflation at all. Samsung has $136 trillion in cash on hand. Hyundai has about 50 trillion won in cash. They are already preparing for deflation, and they already know that cash is one of the best assets in a deflation.

Cash, government bonds, and the Macquarie Infrastructure Fund are cash equivalents. If we look at government bonds, short-term government bonds are very similar to cash, but long-term government bonds are slightly different because they are more sensitive to interest rate changes and are not as freely tradable as short-term government bonds.

Even Mr.Big Investor is now buying short-term Treasuries, but he seems to be cautious about buying long-term Treasuries.

A great opportunity to make a lot of money short selling comes from a long period of decline in the domestic dollar and gold prices. Of course, real estate prices also plummet. This is when cash and cash equivalents are king.

In a long-term deflation, you shouldn't hold dollars outside of the United States. Only cash and cash equivalents should be held. In this case, the dollar becomes property, not cash, and the dollar becomes a monster.

Chapter 15)

New Asset Allocation method (Diamond dollar dichotomy method) The diamond dollar dichotomy doesn't work in long term deflation.

In a long term deflation, there are few investments that will grow your wealth. Cash and cash equivalents, gov. bonds, and a few inverse ETFs.

In a long term deflation,
Stocks collapse first.
Six months later,
apartments collapse,
the dollar collapses,
bitcoin collapses,

gold collapses,

oil, copper, silver, and everything physical collapses.

South Korea collapses by 2029. The rest of the world collapses by 2048.

But whether it's inflation or deflation, we as investors need to grow or protect our wealth.

1) Traditional Assets Allocation

The traditional way to protect your wealth is to divide it into three parts. The idea is that if you divide your wealth into real estate, stocks, and deposits, you can protect your wealth by securing the safety, profitability, and liquidity of all three at the same time. This is the most popular traditional wealth preservation method. This is the traditional asset allocation method.

In other words, 33% real estate + 33% stocks + 33%

deposits will keep your wealth safe, profitable, and liquid. Now, Koreans probably keep more than 90% of their wealth in real estate and less than 10% in stocks or deposits.

Americans are the opposite of Koreans; they and other people in developed countries hold 10% in real estate and 90% in liquid assets, which is now an effective theory only for Americans.

South Korea is the seventh country to join the 3050 club and is now a real, actual developed country. As a country becomes more developed, the proportion of financial assets in its wealth portfolio increases.

There is a phenomenon of money movement into financial assets, usually every 10 years or more. Statistics show that a person's portfolio shifts to financial assets as much as their age.

By the age of 70, 70% of assets are financial assets, which is the asset portfolio of citizens in developed countries. Korea is also a developed country, and its wealth portfolio will gradually change its asset composition.

Simply holding on to the wealth preservation method of the three-wealth rule or the two-wealth rule (50% cash + 50% real estate) to preserve wealth is a method that only works in an inflation economy and is only effective for Americans.

In a long term deflation, wealth in real assets such as real estate, gold, silver, etc. is automatically transferred to holders of cash assets through a process of collapse.

People often argue about whether it's harder to build or

to defend. The author's wealth division method is a way for someone with $500 billion or trillions to keep 100% of their wealth.

2) New Asserts Allocation method:

There is one more traditional wealth preservation method, the wealth dichotomy, which the author created by applying the principles of the Diamond Dollar Investment Method.

The theory is that you can protect your wealth by dividing your wealth into two parts: real estate and cash, stocks, or savings. This traditional wealth dichotomy is much less useful and is not as popular as the wealth triad.

The wealth dichotomy, which is the result of the author's original research, should be called differently than the traditional wealth dichotomy. In order not to confuse people, we will rename it the Diamond Wealth Dichotomy based on the understanding of the Diamond Dollar Investment Method as a wealth preservation method in [Figure 22].

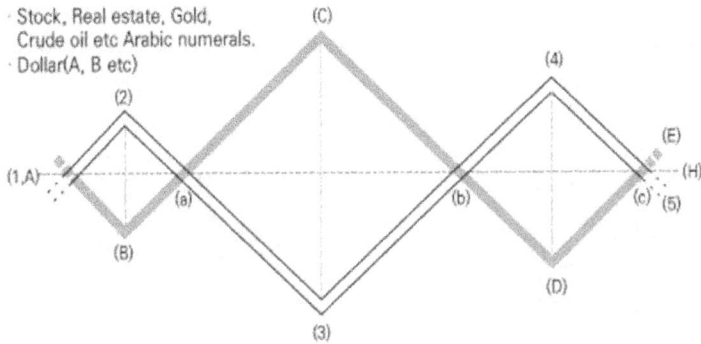

[Fig.22] Understanding the Diamond Dollar Investment Method as a Property Preservation Measure

I.e., the Diamond wealth dichotomy is
It is a method of wealth preservation that allows you to keep 100% of your wealth in any case by dividing your wealth by 50% of dollars and 50% of the sum of your other wealth.

This method is 100% effective in inflation economies and short term deflation periods.

This is a wealth preservation method that applies the principles of the Diamond Dollar Investment Method. This is because the dollar and other assets such as real estate and stocks have an inverse relationship with each other.

In short term deflation, i.e., preserving wealth in normal times, is a simple matter of applying the Diamond Dollar Investment Method.

Of course, the Diamond Wealth Dichotomy is not applicable to people and countries that use the dollar as their everyday currency, i.e., the United States.

Let's first understand the Diamond Dollar Investment Method as a wealth preservation method in [Figure 22]. Arabic numbers such as ①,②, etc. are lines representing the movement of real assets such as stocks, real estate, crude oil, gold, silver, copper, etc. (A),(B), etc. are gray lines representing the movement of the dollar.

The horizontal dotted lines represented by (1,A,H) are the equilibrium points of asset prices corresponding to each dollar price. They can be called equilibrium price lines.

First, if we look at the price of the dollar moving along the gray line, we can see that as the dollar price falls from point (A) to point (B), the prices of the goods represented by Arabic numerals, such as stocks, apartments, gold, crude oil, etc.

After that, we can see that the dollar price and the price of a good are at equilibrium at point (a) on the equilibrium line.
For the same good, we can see that the real price of the

good fluctuates more violently as the dollar price fluctuates, as evidenced by the largest diamond in the center.

However, as the dollar price increases, the price of the good decreases, and eventually, the dollar price and the price of the good are in equilibrium at point (b), which is the equilibrium price line.

In this way, the prices of the goods are constantly moving slightly according to the dollar price, either due to a financial crisis or a simple spontaneous rebound, and the prices always converge to the equilibrium line.

This always happens in short term deflation and never happens in long term deflation, i.e. all goods and the dollar collapse. This is the phenomenon of long term deflation.

This is what happens after the BC'② line in [Figure 2]. You can see it in the graph of Japan's lost 30 years.

It can be seen that it is easier to make money or to keep money, but it is more difficult to accumulate money. This is because keeping money is so perfectly and simply secured by the Diamond wealth dichotomy.

It's time to throw out traditional property preservation methods.

The four most common safe-haven assets are gold, the dollar, the franc, and the yen. Safe assets are assets that investors prefer when the value of their property is not safe, i.e. when the asset market is unstable.

Right now, with the price of gold floating in the air, it seems like the world and Koreans alike are favoring gold as a safe haven asset.

However, in the long term deflation, the price of gold will eventually collapse. Gold is currently about 80% above its normal price, with evidence that it is overvalued, as we will explain later.

It is important to note that during inflation (i.e. short term deflation), the Diamond Wealth Dichotomy still applies, but during long term deflation (i.e. three years or more), such as Japan's, the Diamond Wealth Dichotomy does not work.

This wealth dichotomy will protect 100% of your wealth, but it will not increase your wealth. However, it is a useful wealth preservation method if you are choosing between money accumulation and money recession.

The world, including Korea, has already entered a long term deflation in January 2016. Whether it is a short term deflation or a long term deflation, cash is the strongest currency in deflation.

It can be cash itself or cash equivalents. There are Macquarie Infrastructure Funds and gov. bonds that are both cash and cash equivalents and generate income.

Recently, KODEX Inverse and other inverse ETFs such as gov. bonds, gold, grains, etc. have been created. By utilizing inverse ETFs such as gov. bonds, grains, crude oil, and the dollar, you can profit from long term deflation, when all prices fall.

Before the creation of inverse ETFs, there was really nothing to invest in during deflation. Stocks, apartments, gold, crude oil, and anything else of value would collapse in price, and unlike institutions, retail investors were not allowed to short sell, i.e. they had no way to react.

The price of Macquarie Infrastructure Fund and gov. bonds will spontaneously jump to the sky depending on the rate of interest rate cut, because the standard interest rate will continue to fall a lot for the next 30 years or more, like Japan, throughout the long term deflation.

It is important to remember that the standard interest rates on govt bonds in Japan and other Western countries have been cut to even negative rates.

Japan exited long term deflation around December 2020, and the world believes that it entered long term deflation in January 2016. Therefore, it is very likely that Korea will remain in long term deflation until 2029 and the rest of the world until 2043.

In Japan, housing prices have collapsed by 80-90% and

stocks by 80% during long term deflation, i.e., unlike in normal times, the diamond-dollar dichotomy cannot protect your wealth during long term deflation. Only cash and cash equivalents will protect your wealth.

Chapter 16)

If it becomes long term deflation, dollar, stocks and real estate collapses

If you invest in anything during a long term deflation, you will lose money and be a fool.

There are three or four reasons for this, but the strongest reason is that the dollar price will continue to collapse in a long term deflation.

The reasons and consequences can be deduced by analyzing Japan first. In the 1970s and 1980s, Japan was the world's leading manufacturing nation, with a huge trade surplus every year and no way to control its money,

The collapse of the domestic dollar in Japan

At the time, the dollar had collapsed in Japan, so Japanese stocks and apartments should have risen dramatically during the same period according to the Diamond Dollar investment method.

Instead, Japanese stocks and apartments collapsed.
Japan has been in a long term deflation state since December 1988, so stocks and apartments in Japan collapsed along with the dollar. In this way, if a country is in a long term deflation, its dollar will collapse throughout the duration of the long term deflation.

No one has been able to explain this phenomenon. The reasons for this have already been explained in the previous chapters. Anyone who buys dollar deposits or invests in overseas dividend stocks or overseas growth stocks now, knowing that a long term deflation has already arrived in Korea in 2016 and has only just begun, is a fool.

Some experts and financial firms are urging you to invest abroad now. Almost everyone who believes them and goes abroad, i.e. buys dollars, is quite unaware that it is death.
.

Consider the following example
1) Let's say that 1$=1200 won at the time of deposit (overseas investment) in dollars.

To deposit (overseas investment) $1000 in dollars, you need $1000 x 1200 won = 1.2 million won in Korean money.
.2) After that, let's say that 1$=800 won when you cancel the dollar deposit or bring the overseas invested dollars into Korea.

To get back the original 1,200,000 won, the dollar deposit or overseas stocks invested must be worth 1,200,000 * 800 = 1500 dollars.

This is a 33.3% loss due to exchange rate alone.

.In order to succeed with dollar investment, i.e. overseas investment, contrary to the above example, the dollar must continue to rise (Won to dollar weakness) or the local invested stock, apartment, etc. must rise.

Of course, if there is a gain, capital gains tax must also be excluded.

Only if these three conditions are met will your gold, dollar deposits, and overseas stock investments be successful. If you can't do well in domestic stocks, how can you succeed in overseas investments where you have to match overseas stock prices and dollar exchange rates at the same time?

Inevitably, the curse of the won comes. Don't go overseas. Don't buy dollars is the answer. When some people say don't buy dollars, you protest that you are buying overseas stocks, not dollars, but you should know that when you buy stocks or apartments abroad, you are buying overseas assets by exchanging dollars, so you are buying dollars and buying overseas stocks at the same time.

There was a news that securities companies that invested in overseas real estate, overseas REITs, and overseas stocks suffered huge losses.In Korea, they are institutional investors, but when they go to developed markets such as the United States, Korean professional investment institutions are only at the level of ants. Even uneducated professionals are always victimized by overseas investment.

With the huge amount of dollars released so far, the world is showing a temporary inflationary phenomenon, so some readers may say that we are in inflation now, and the author is talking about deflation at the wrong time, such as short term deflation, ,long term deflation, which makes no sense.

However, you should always read between the lines when it comes to the economy.

All investments should be made with a view to tomorrow, not today. After the temporary strengthening of the dollar, which will coincide with the US QT, the global economy will crash as the dollar recovers, i.e. tightening.

According to the theory of Yale professor Robert Triffin, it has already been proven that reducing the dollar pushes the world deeper into a deflation spiral. This is known as Triffin's dilemma. It is called Triffin's dilemma.

In a long term deflation, the dollar becomes more of a property than a monetary instrument. In a long term deflation, the dollar turns into a monster.

This long term deflation is almost impossible to cure in a short period of time like Japan. The causes of long term deflation are completely different from short term deflation, mainly because they have a long term impact. A weaker dollar, demographic problems, debt, etc. are not short-term fixes.

Investing in dollars in a long term deflation country is a guarantee of failure, so even if you invest abroad, you will suffer huge exchange rate losses when you bring your money back home.

The collapse of the Nikkei

Then Japan was forced to sign the Plaza Accord in 1985. The price of the dollar in Japan started to fall in the 1970s. In other words, the yen had been strong since the 1970s.

On September 22, 1985, the price of the dollar in Japan

collapsed from 240 yen to 140 yen in one morning.

And then, just when you thought it was over, the U.S. dollar collapsed to 76.34 yen in Japan over the next 30 years. Japanese stocks and apartments had a chance to skyrocket, because according to the Diamond Dollar Investment Method, the price of the dollar is inversely proportional to the price of stocks, apartments, gold and silver.

But that's not what happened. Everything just went down. It was a strange phenomenon. No economist or economic research center could explain this phenomenon for 30 years.

All you had to do in Japan was invest in stocks, real estate, anything, and it went down. As the dollar continued to fall, all assets in Japan collapsed in price. But that's not what happened. The dollar kept falling, and Japan's Nikkei index and land prices kept falling.

The collapse of land myths.

The land myth that land, or real estate, can only go up, started to collapse overnight, i.e., after the Plaza Accord, housing prices started to fall, which led to the land myth that land prices were going up all the time.

But when the long term deflation happened, it wasn't. It kept going down. He was paying rent, and a year later, the price of the house was lower than the amount I was paying in rent. This happened every year, so He invested in the U.S. like everyone else.

If you invested in anything in Japan, it went down. After investing in the U.S.,He thought He did really well for the first few years. Everyone else was betting on the U.S. market, including apartments. Eventually, He realized that if the dollar started to rise again, he could make a lot of money.

So the investor's money went overseas and was not brought back into Japan for 30 years due to exchange losses. The author calls these funds "ghost dollars".

No one quite realized that this deflation would last for 32 years: 32 years of falling prices and flat salaries. This is the long term deflation phenomenon.

No one in the world has studied this long term deflation properly. I don't think it's possible to have a long term deflation that lasts more than three years in the human world.

The Japanese phenomenon is not common, it's unique to Japan, and we think they must be doing something wrong.

But no. The author first defined deflation for more than three years as long term deflation, which is almost impossible to cure in a short period of time like Japan. The causes of long term deflation are completely different from short term deflation.

First of all, the outcome is that investing in the dollar is a guarantee of failure. In a long term deflation, the relationship between the dollar and the price of stocks and apartments changes from an inverse relationship to a proportional relationship.

Therefore, after 32 years of dollar depreciation in Japan, Japanese stocks and apartments collapsed by 80-90%.

In December 2012, Abenomics continued Japan's money printing, and now the yen/dollar exchange rate fluctuates around 150 yen. Japan emerged from long term deflation in December 2020, and the Nikkei is at a record high.

In the end, I concluded,

It was a very strange phenomenon. No one could have predicted it. There was no opportunity to sell stocks and buy dollars like in short term deflation.

This is when Japan began its long term deflation, which still has the same proportional relationship between the dollar and stock prices. The main phenomenon of long term deflation is that the dollar collapses and stock prices and apartments also collapse.

As the dollar collapses, gold also falls and everything else in the world collapses according to the time-lagged gold investment method. The gold investment theory was created. It is a five-month time lag gold investment method.

At that time, the dollar collapsed in Japan, so Japanese stocks and apartments should have risen at the same rate according to the Diamond Dollar Investment Method.

However, Japanese stocks and apartments collapsed instead. Japan has been in a long term deflation state since December 1988, so stocks and apartments collapsed in tandem with the decline of the dollar in Japan.

When a country is in a long term deflation, its dollar will collapse throughout the duration of the deflation.

Gold follows the time-lagged gold investment method and collapses in line with the trend of the dollar five months ago. In other words, if you invest in gold or the dollar during a long term deflation, you will lose money and be a fool.

Anyone who signs up for dollar deposits or invests in overseas dividend stocks or overseas growth stocks now, knowing that the long term deflation has already arrived in Korea in 2016 and has only just begun, is a fool.

Amateurish professionals and financial firms are urging you to invest overseas now. Almost everyone who believes them and goes overseas, i.e. buys dollars, is quite unaware that it is death.

.So, if you don't react differently from the masses, no one will survive like the Japanese, i.e., you should keep in mind that if you invest in dollars and gold now, you will lose money and become a fool.

In a long term deflation, the dollar will become just property rather than cash. Of course, in the United States, the dollar is always cash.

People outside the country should not hold dollars in a long term deflation. This is when the dollar becomes more property than cash. In a long term deflation, outside of the US, the dollar becomes a monster.

Chapter 17)

If it becomes long term deflation, bitcoin and gold will collapse too!

Bitcoin rightfully collapses

People think that holding Bitcoin instead of dollars will have many of the same effects as holding dollars. Gold has risen about 200% more than the dollar index for no good reason. Now, the only thing left for these assets to do is collapse.

We'll soon see that the price of gold and bitcoin have been, in a word, nonsense. Simply put, gold is an inflation-proof investment, not a deflationary one.

Bitcoin is essentially worthless and will eventually converge to zero. Let's take it one step by one.

There are many reasons for this, but the biggest cause of the collapse in the short term is the listing of physical Bitcoin ETFs, which now have the advantage of anonymity, which is the same as the abolition of the secrecy of Swiss banks in the past.

On January 10, 2024, a Bitcoin spot EFT was listed on the American Stock Exchange, i.e., it is the same as the listing of Bitcoin spot.

Going forward, when the spot price of Bitcoin goes up or down, the Bitcoin ETF listed on the US stock exchanges will move accordingly. i.e. Bitcoin ETFs are like gold ETFs or silver ETFs. In other words, you can own Bitcoin indirectly, just like gold or silver.

In the meantime, Bitcoin is expensive for no good reason: it's anonymous, it exists only online, it's portable, and it's free. Bitcoin is a safe haven for political money, bribes, and tax evasion. From an asset class perspective, there is no reason to hold Bitcoin.

I.e., buying a Bitcoin spot ETF is the same as buying the spot. The whole point of holding Bitcoin was its anonymity, and now that that advantage is gone, the demand for Bitcoin spot is bound to decrease.

Eventually, the demand for bitcoin spot will disappear over time, and eventually bitcoin spot will collapse and disappear.

Bitcoin is recognized as a virtual asset because it is listed as a spot ETF on the American Stock Exchange, not because it is a virtual currency. Make no mistake,

Bitcoin is not a currency, i.e., it has no asset value to the average person, except for some holders.

Bitcoin has no function as a currency at all, but because people buy and sell it for money, i.e. people recognize it as an asset, it is recognized as a virtual asset with asset value.

The U.S. Securities and Exchange Commission (SEC) will now be able to see at a glance the trading history and holdings of Bitcoin spot ETFs by investor entity. In the end, the desire to hold Bitcoin for purely investment purposes can be solved by holding it indirectly.

There's no reason for investors to hold Bitcoin spot directly because they know who owns how much. As a result, the demand for anonymity and confidentiality of transactions, which are the reasons why Bitcoin is expensive, collapses as the share of simple holders increases.

With the listing of Bitcoin spot ETFs, investors have an easier way to invest in Bitcoin indirectly, which naturally reduces the demand for Bitcoin spot, which in turn causes the price to collapse.

Another reason why Bitcoin is bound to collapse is the recent success of the discovery of superconducting materials by South Korea's Quantum Energy Research Institute.

Bitcoin has a halving date of April 2024, and the vague expectation that the price of Bitcoin will increase further is the discovery of a superconductor that costs almost nothing to produce, i.e., it costs almost nothing to produce. that makes Bitcoin worthless.

With the discovery of superconducting materials, the

cost of electricity and the price of crude oil will converge to almost zero in the future, and the only reason bitcoin is expensive is that it requires a lot of electricity to produce, which is the cost of mining.

Other virtual assets still have near-zero production costs. Therefore, the price of all virtual assets will converge to zero.

Since Bitcoin is the leader, it is only natural that other digital coin assets will also converge to zero, so it is only natural that Bitcoin will collapse and be removed from the market in the future.

This is because the cost of production is zero, and anyone can create and sell cryptocurrency without any restrictions. Accordingly, it is natural that the price of Ethereum and many other cryptocurrencies will converge to zero and disappear.

Again, Bitcoin, Ethereum, etc. are not cryptocurrencies, but virtual assets, which have no role and will have no asset value in the future.

In some cases, bitcoin has even replaced the exchange function of the dollar. There are now spot ETFs, i.e. bitcoin spot, so you can buy and sell them directly.

If Bitcoin is accepted as a currency, there is no control over the inflow and outflow of foreign currency, and illegal money can be exchanged for free.

In addition, currency issuance is a huge profit and interest business for governments. If the government decides that bitcoins are money, it will completely liberalize the money printing business. It is the business of turning paper into money. This can never happen.

Furthermore, Bitcoin does not fulfill many of the requirements for legal tender. Furthermore, it would be a free transfer of power to the issuers of Bitcoin and other cryptocurrencies, which would monopolize the signorage effect enjoyed by governments.

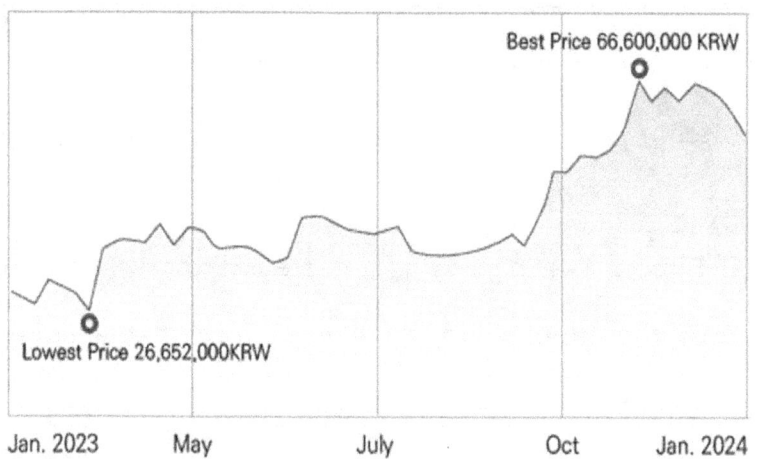

[Figure.23] Bitcoin price.KRW(Feb. 2024) courtesy of NAVER.

This leads to a funny phenomenon, i.e., anyone can print money. Before the Great Depression, central banks were private enterprises, but it's awkward for a private enterprise to issue legal tender. Governments can't give away the benefits of fiat currency for free under any circumstances.

It's the magic that turns paper into money. The manufacturing cost of a $100 bill or a $10 bill is about the same, close to zero.

It's a big business with margins of hundreds or thousands of percent. Therefore, privately issued cryptocurrencies such as Bitcoin will not be able to compete with the government's forced acceptance of digital currencies anytime soon.

Bitcoin is not a medium of exchange, a means of payment, a store of value, or a measure of value, which are the four main functions of money. In short, Bitcoin does not fulfill the functions of money.

With the exception of the blockchain function to keep

track of bitcoin holdings, transactions, etc. In the future, only CBDC (Central Bank digital currency) issued by the central banks of each country will exist as digital currencies.

In the future, government-issued digital currencies combined with blockchain technology will be 100% visible to the government. If countries use only digital currencies, black money will be eliminated from the world at once.

Money laundering, terrorist financing, tax evasion, and online gambling would be eradicated. The US dominates international payments with the dollar and uses exclusion from the dollar payment network as a sanction against nations it disagrees with.

Central bank digital currencies (CBDCs) will also work to stimulate the economy through negative standard interest rates. So far, negative standard interest rates have failed to stimulate consumption, but digital currencies can cause governments to print less money if left unused.

As such, the idea of holding bitcoin as a substitute for the dollar when its very existence is uncertain is, in a word, nonsense.

In addition, as long term deflation will soon be in full swing, all valuable things in the world will be destroyed, so even if Bitcoin and cryptocurrency, which are representative of cryptocurrency, become worthless.

Gold also collapses.

Gold follows the same track of the dollar as it did 5 months ago, following the time-lagged gold investment method, and collapses. In other words, if you invest in dollar stocks apartments bitcoin gold during a long term deflation, you lose money and become a fool.

Collapse of the domestic gold price

Since the outbreak of long term deflation, the dollar and gold have

1) became proportional to each other

2) There is a 5 month time lag between the two for the first time. The gold investment method that applies this principle is the "5 month time lag gold investment method."

Therefore, the time lag gold investment method is a unique gold investment method that can be utilized in the long term deflation period summarized by the author.

In normal times, i.e. short term deflation, gold moves in opposite direction to the dollar, so you should sell gold when the dollar goes up and buy gold when the dollar goes down, in line with the Diamond Dollar Investment Method.

However, in a long term deflation, gold follows the same price track as the dollar five months ago. In [Figure 15], we can see that the price of gold follows the track of the dollar index price five months ago.

In the event of short term deflation, the dollar rises sharply, stock prices fall sharply, and circular buying and selling begins.

The vertical dotted line in [Figure 13], the vertical dotted line indicating January 2016 in [Figure 14], and (A) in [Figure 15], i.e., from January 2016, the author believes that long term deflation has arrived in Korea and the world.

After January 2016 through these three figures, we see that the dollar price and gold price rise together in a proportional relationship, and we conclude that long term deflation has begun.i.e., we can see that we should not buy and sell according to the Diamond Dollar Investment Method after January 2016.

The vertical dotted line is the dividing line between short term deflation (=depression, inflationary economic period) and long term deflation, i.e., from now on, the rules for investing in gold and the dollar should be reversed: as prices rise, the price of gold rises at the same time.

After seeing this, it would be a huge error of judgment to think that the price of gold will continue to rise indefinitely. What we have seen in Japan, which has experienced long term deflation in the past, is that the price of the U.S. dollar collapses in countries with long term deflation.

It would be foolish to invest in the U.S. dollar now, and it would be foolish to invest in gold now because we know that when the dollar goes down, the price of gold goes down.

And when the price of the U.S. dollar increases, all prices increase indiscriminately, resulting in inflation. On the other hand, if the dollar is constantly falling, all domestic prices will fall, resulting in deflation. The current gold price is an extreme abnormal phenomenon.

Second, gold is not a safe haven asset. In a long term deflation, the dollar collapses first and gold follows the same track five months later. The US in 1929 and Japan in 1989, or more precisely since December 1988, were in long term deflation.

Since January 2016, Korea and the rest of the world have been in long term deflation. One of the most powerful causes of long term deflation is the persistent weakness of the dollar, which soon develops into a strong dollar bear market.

In a long term deflation situation, when the dollar goes down, the KOSPI goes down, and when the dollar goes up, the KOSPI goes up. The relationship between the dollar and stocks, apartments, gold, silver, etc. goes from inverse to proportional.

Since Korea and other countries have not yet experienced a long term deflation, the proportional relationship is not obvious, so we can see it in [Figure 2], which shows the domestic US dollar price in Japan since December 1988, i.e. the yen-dollar index and the Nikkei stock index.

In long term deflation, the dollar price declines consistently over the long term, as it did in Japan. Gold tracks the price of the dollar from five months ago, so international gold is also destined to collapse. This is because the world has been in a long term deflation since January 2016.

Consider the data below for a moment.
Dollar Index:
January 2016: 115.9
February 2023: 121.5
4.83% increase
.

International gold price:
January 2016: 381.9
February 2023: 671.3
75.8% increase
.

In the roughly eight years from 2016 to 2023, the international dollar price, i.e. the Dollar Index, rose by

4.83%.

In contrast, the international gold price surged 75.8% during the same period. Since January 2016, the world has been in a long term deflation, yet the gold price has so far outperformed the dollar price by an excessive 70.9% (75.8-4.83=70.9%).

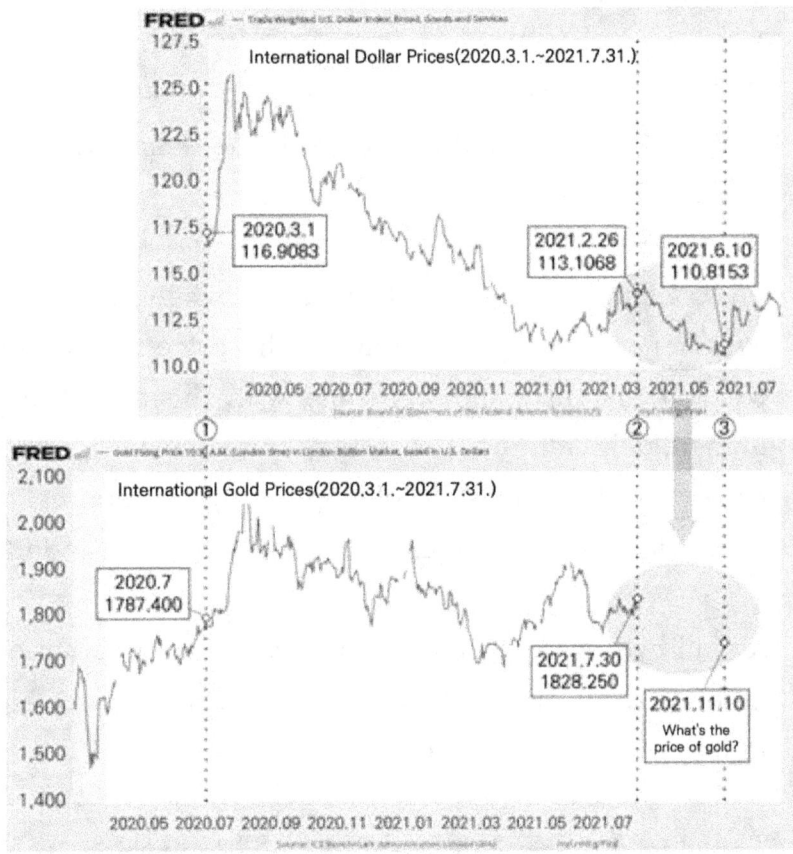

[Fig.24] Forecast of future international gold prices after

Aug 1, 2021

The price of the dollar in Japan has been falling on average, the Nikkei index has been falling, and Japanese real estate has been falling dramatically. Unfortunately, I don't have a graph of the price of gold in Japan, so I can't make a direct comparison.

However, we can infer that the price of gold in Japan has probably followed the price of the dollar with a lag of about 5 months.

In conclusion, it is clear that when a country experiences long term deflation, the price of the dollar will fall in that country. In line with this, stock prices immediately fall by the same percentage, apartment prices lag the domestic dollar price by six months, and gold prices lag the domestic dollar price by five months.

All fall by the same percentage. In addition, international and domestic prices of other commodities also collapse in line with the dollar price.

Applying this, we can see that since January 2016, you shouldn't invest in gold, silver, crude oil, copper, or any other commodity, even internationally.

As the saying goes, there is no more powerful domestic price decline, i.e. deflationary factor, than a decline in the domestic price of the dollar.

The most powerful factor that depresses all domestic prices is the constant depreciation of the dollar. A steady decline in the dollar is a must in a country with long term deflation.

Assets such as apartments, gold, crude oil, silver, etc. always lag the domestic dollar price by 6 months in countries with long term deflation, so you can safely trade futures and short these assets.

This is a very important, proven fact.
This is something that no one has ever explained to me or guided me through. This is the credit of the author of the world's first full-scale analysis of long term deflation.

In fact, Japan's lost 30 years were caused by a trade surplus that lasted for three decades. It goes without saying that buying gold as a safe haven right now is a foolish investment.

If you're investing in gold futures, you should consider it time to sell if you have to raise your margin more than once or twice.

The slightest reduction in leverage is a big shock to institutional investors and they should get out. Gold is leveraged at about 20x.

Recently, gold and Bitcoin have been experiencing a strange phenomenon of increasing correlation. Neither is an investment.

Even according to traditional theory, gold is an inflationary, not deflationary, hedge against inflation.

Nor is gold a yield-generating asset in and of itself. Finally, we emphasize once again that in a long term deflation, gold is an unconditionally down asset. Gold is not a safe haven asset.

In deflationary times, cash, deposits, and cash equivalents are safe haven assets. Even government bonds, which are supposedly risk free assets, are not. This appears to be an excessive demand for gold that will soon be corrected.

[[Figure 16] is a graph that shows the price of gold against the dollar price 5 months ahead in order to more closely compare the price difference over a 5-month time horizon, i.e. to predict the price of gold after July 30, 2021.

Then, the international price of the dollar, i.e. the dollar index price, is the price of gold 5 months later. While the price of gold five months later is not exactly proportional to the dollar price, the trend is almost 100% consistent.

In addition to the proportional relationship between the dollar index and the gold price, we can see that the gold price follows the trajectory of the dollar price already recorded about five months ago.

Compare the previous graph of the dollar index with the graph of the international gold price in [Figure 24].

Isn't it amazing?

These two graphs are indistinguishable, and if you utilize them, your gold investing will be a pleasure. Investing in gold will be as easy as treading water in the future.

[Figure 25] is a long term graph that we took to verify whether the international dollar index and international gold prices in November 2021 moved as predicted in [Figure 24].

Since the gold price follows the track of the dollar price by five months, the September 30, 2022 date shown in the dollar index graph above becomes February 2024, as shown in the vertical dotted line ② in the international gold price graph below.

This graph compares the two graphs by adjusting the

start date by 5 months. This method is the best way to invest in gold with a 5 month time lag, and it is also an accurate and simple way to capture the long term deflation that has hit the world. All are the author's original diagnostics.

The vertical dotted line ① is the actual international gold price on November 10, 2021, which is the line in the graph below [Figure 25]. It can be seen that the price has followed the price of the international dollar, i.e. the Daler Index, five months ago.

As we have verified many times, the international gold price will follow the track of the dollar and collapse in February 2024, lagging the dollar price by 5 months, as shown in [Figure 25].

In [Chapter 12], I explained how to invest during a long term deflation. At that time, I emphasized that since we are in a long term deflation, you should never invest in gold, bitcoin, or the dollar. Now, let's look at a graph to see why.

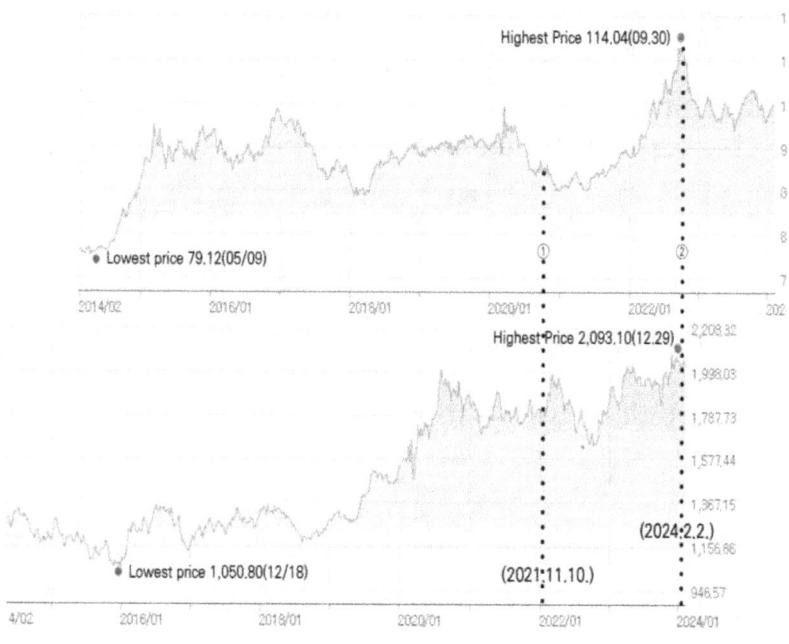

[Fig. 25] Trend of dollar index and international gold price from 2014.2~ 2024.1 (10 years) (Naver)

The graph above [Figure 25] is a graph of the dollar

index over the 10 year period from February 2014 to January 2024, and the graph below is a graph of the international gold price over the same period, i.e. from February 2014 to January 2024.

First of all, in the above graph of the international dollar price, the date of the 10 year high of the dollar price is 114.04 on September 30, 2022.

The 10 year high for the international gold price is 2,093.10 on December 29, 2022, which is still three months away. The date and amount of the lowest dollar price is $79.12 on May 9, 2014, shown earlier in [Figure 25].

Meanwhile, the lowest gold price is on December 10, 2014, with a price of $1,050.80. Calculating the time difference, we see that the international gold price followed the international dollar price about six months later.

I.e., six months, not five months as claimed by the author, leaving a time lag of about one month. Since then, both the Dollar Index price and the international gold price have increased.

This suggests that it is reasonable to use the price movements of the Dollar Index as an indicator for buying and selling international gold.

At this point, there is actually a three-month lag between the dates of the dollar and gold's respective peaks, rather than a five month lag. This suggests that the gold price will reach its lowest point in February 2024, two months from now.

Since September 30, 2022, the Dollar Index price has decreased by 114.04-103.99 = $10.05 (about 8.8%).

Meanwhile, the international gold price has decreased by 2,093.10-2,038.70 = 54.4 (2.59%) since December 29, 2022. It is very likely that the international gold price will collapse and hit a new low in February.

The 5-month lag between the dollar index and the international gold price can be used to predict and trade the international gold price, i.e., it can be used as a technique to trade the dollar and gold during long term deflation.

It is not known why the international dollar price and the international gold price move along the same trajectory five months later. Nor do the authors know why it is possible to use this technique to accurately time the onset of long term deflation.

This is something that economic researchers and

academics will have to study in the future, but we as investors are already aware of these changes, so if we invest accordingly, we can hit the jackpot without making mistakes.

In 2016, the world has already experienced a long term deflation, and I think the world is not yet in the full swing of long term deflation like Japan, but if you look at [Figure 14] and [Figure 15],
the world is much more advanced in long term deflation than Korea because the dollar and gold are already in a proportional relationship, and Korea is still using the Diamond dollar investment method.

It is important to remember one important fact here.
That is, during a long term deflation, the gold price and the dollar price will move in the same direction and trajectory with a lag of about 5 months, but the rate of increase and decrease of the international gold price will

not move in exact proportion to each other.

This appears to be an irrational excess of demand for gold. However, like Bitcoin's collapse, it is likely to be corrected: gold has outperformed the rise in the dollar index by about 70.9%.

This suggests that the international gold price will collapse by about 70.9% in the future. People have been looking for a place to

invest using the trial-and-error method, and they are wrong to choose gold.

Investing in gold during a long term deflation period is just stupid. Gold is an inflation-proof asset, not a deflation-proof asset. Moreover, the current deflation is not a short term deflation, but a long term deflation, in which all commodities collapse and collapse and collapse.

As predicted in [Chapter 16] and [Chapter 17], in a long term deflation, everything that is valuable on the asset class, such as the dollar, stocks, real estate, bitcoin, gold, etc. will collapse in price.

We saw this in the US in the 1930s and Japan in 1989. The author cannot prove the actual price movements of Bitcoin or gold in any of these cases because he does not have the relevant data, but as I have explained throughout the book, if you look at the characteristic features of long term deflation that move in proportion to the dollar, every asset on the planet will collapse in price. Only gov't bonds ignite a spectacular rise, i.e. the answer is the same.

(Part Three)
Japan is no longer a Long Term Deflation country

By 2043, the wealth of those who did not respond to deflation over the next 20 years will have shrunk by 10~20%. Meanwhile, those who responded with deflation-beating investment vehicles will see their wealth grow four to tenfold.

The inflation that begins around 2043 will last another nearly 70 years. Meanwhile, the period just before the new inflation begins is also the optimal time for real estate owners who have endured the collapse without being able to sell.

After all, having experienced the ultra-long term deflation that came to Korea around 2013 (or 2016) and continued until around 2043, it is no wonder that the public does not realize that we have returned to an inflationary economy again.

As I explained in "Korean Tears (How Salarymen and Poor People Get Rich by Only Passing on to Their Children)", the point at which the Diamond Dollar Investment Method does not work is the beginning of a long term deflation economy, and the point at which the Diamond Dollar Investment Method begins to work is the return to an inflationary economy.

Korea's long term deflation lasted from 2013 (or 2016) to 2043 (or 2043), and it is expected that the country will finally return to an inflationary economy in 2043 (or 2045), 20 years later. As already mentioned, it will be when the debt ratio of each individual is reduced to about 100%, as confirmed by the Diamond Dollar Investment Method.

The order of investment will again be first-class enterprises, i.e. stocks of new industry leaders, and first-class real estate. Gold is a long way off from the cumulative effects of inflation, so don't even bother looking at it for the time being.

Existing wealth that is not handled properly will go through stages of decline and migration and be reborn as someone else's wealth. Wealth is primarily transferred to those who hold cash.

The state has no interest. Inflation and deflation are not transfers of national wealth to foreign countries, but only transfers between classes of people.

Deflation seemed to disappear with the outbreak of World War II, although no one knows for sure. Starting in 1945, inflation lasted for a whole 70 years, which meant that even if you held real assets such as real estate or stocks, your wealth only increased with inflation.

Now, the world is in the midst of a long term deflation that has already begun, although it varies slightly depending on the country, and it is likely that we will not enter an inflationary economy again until 2043.

If you time the next inflation period correctly and hold your real assets, such as apartments or stocks, for the next 70 years, you will be wealthy again.

So it is very important to be interested in the current deflationary economy and make deflation-beating investments in time for the next inflationary period, i.e., to get rich in time for another inflationary period.
This is the biggest reason to study deflation, especially long term deflation, in advance.

Until now, no economist, economic research institute, or national institute has studied deflation in a systematic way and divided it into short term deflation, which is a normal economic fluctuation, and long term deflation, which lasts for more than five years.

Only the author categorizes deflation into short term deflation (5 years or less) and long term deflation (5 years or less).

The author advocated, verified and proved that investments should be completely different accordingly. Therefore, if you invest according to the investment method in this book, you will get rich.

At this time, Japan seized the opportunity. However, the Japanese government has a debt-to-GDP ratio of 248%. It is by far the highest among OECD countries. This means that the government can't afford to be fiscally liberal.

Now that Japan has a chance to escape long term deflation with a massive monetary easing policy, it should choose a surefire way to return to economic sanity.

This is the sale of Japanese state-owned property.
At a time when real estate prices in Japan are rising, the government should sell excess or unneeded state-owned property to Japanese citizens or Japanese enterprises to pay off the gov's debt in a short period of time. This is the only way to turn the broken economy around.

Bring the debt ratio back to the average debt ratio of OECD countries. This will be Japan's chance to completely exit long term deflation. It is actually the way out of a long term deflation state.

It is important to keep in mind that all debt, i.e. debt, whether it is personal, enterprise, or government, is not eliminated until it is paid. Japan should also not forget that a persistent and excessive trade surplus is also a long term cause of deflation.

Japan is a net borrower, investing about twice its GDP abroad. This excessive overseas investment also reduces domestic consumption, which could be one of the causes of long term deflation.

Chapter 18)

Long term deflation of the Japan i.e,
Japan's Collapse and Revive... and Beyond

If we analyze the events so far, Abenomics was successful in December 2020. The proof of success is that the Yen-Dollar and Nikkei indices have reversed their inverse relationship from a direct correlation to an inverse relationship.

Japan has now been out of long term deflation for exactly 32 years (December 1989-December 2020) since it entered long term deflation in December 1989. and reverted to the normal economic state of short-term deflation.

Japanese tears, shed for 32 years, need not be shed

anymore. The author is only now realizing that Japan has escaped long term deflation, but Mr.Big Investor is already investing in Japan. What a great guy. How did he know?

Whether it's a hunch or a premonition, or he has proof, Mr.Big Investor is investing in Japan, he's a great guy.
Now you have to buy Japan to make money. Mr.Big Investor first invested in Japan's five major conglomerates - Mitsubishi, Itochu, Mitsui, Sumitomo, and Marubeni - in August 2020, and reportedly did so with loans from Japan.

In the author's opinion, Japan did not escape long term deflation until December 2020, and Mr.Big Investor bought Japan before it was confirmed by indicators.

In other words, Mr.Big Investor may have had other means to confirm whether Japan had exited the long-term deflation, but he bought Japan on a hunch(?) without checking, and he was right.

Perhaps, if he had confirmed Japan's escape from long term deflation in indicators and data, he would have acted upon the announcement. This is because on February 22, 2024, the Nikkei 225 Index surpassed the Nikkei's peak index of 38.915 on January 4, 1990, just before Japan's long term deflation began in earnest.

On February 22, 2024, the Nikkei 225 was at 39,156, meaning that Japan is now completely out of long term deflation.

As of the end of February 2024, the interest rate on loans in Japan is still around 0%, and the average dividend of Japanese conglomerates is around 5%. In other words, in terms of interest rates, M.Big Investor has already locked in profits and invested.

The reason why Japanese people were not investing in Japanese stocks, even though the math showed a 5% annualized gain, was because the average price of all Nikkei stocks fell by more than 5% per year.

In other words, it was inevitable that the yen-dollar depreciation would lead to exchange losses, turning investments into ghost dollars that would never return home. After more than 30 years of long term deflation, there was nothing to invest in in Japan.

The Japanese had been making rational investments in their own right. Now, Japan has become a normalized economy where financial technology is possible even if they don't invest abroad and invest domestically.

Mr.Big Investor has been increasing his stake in Japan General Trading Company every year. If the shares he already owns hold up, he'll earn about 5% a year. The Japanese economy is now back in a virtuous cycle. Now is the time to invest in

Japan.

In the author's opinion, Japan is already out of long term deflation, which means that it is much more favorable to invest in export conglomerates now that the country is in a period of high exchange rates.

Recall that in the author's opinion, Japan is already free of long term deflation, which means that it is much more profitable to invest in exporting conglomerates in the future because of the high exchange rate, which was discussed in detail in the previous chapter on exchange rate policy.

One thing to consider is the yen-dollar exchange rate. In the first place, overseas investments should be made in countries where the local currency is strong.

Only then you can enjoy exchange rate gains. Of course, Mr.Big Investor probably invested in Japan because he believed that the yen-dollar exchange rate is weak now, but will be strong again in a few years.

The economic community believes that Japan's long term deflation began in January 1990. However, the author wrote a few years ago that Japan's long term deflation began in December 1989. This author argued several years ago with the first publication of [Figure 2].

The standard for determining whether a country has entered a long-tern deflation is whether the relationship between the domestic exchange rate and the domestic stock index is inversely or directly related.

In [Figure 2], the vertical dotted lines BC'② are the boundaries of Japan's transition from short-term deflation to long-term deflation.

The vertical dotted line BC'② is December 1989, indicating that before this line, Japan was in a short-term deflationary state, and after this line, Japan was in a long-term deflationary state.

If you compare the yen-dollar graph and the Nikkei index before the vertical dotted line BC'②, you can see that the Nikkei index is rising sharply as the yen-dollar exchange rate is falling.

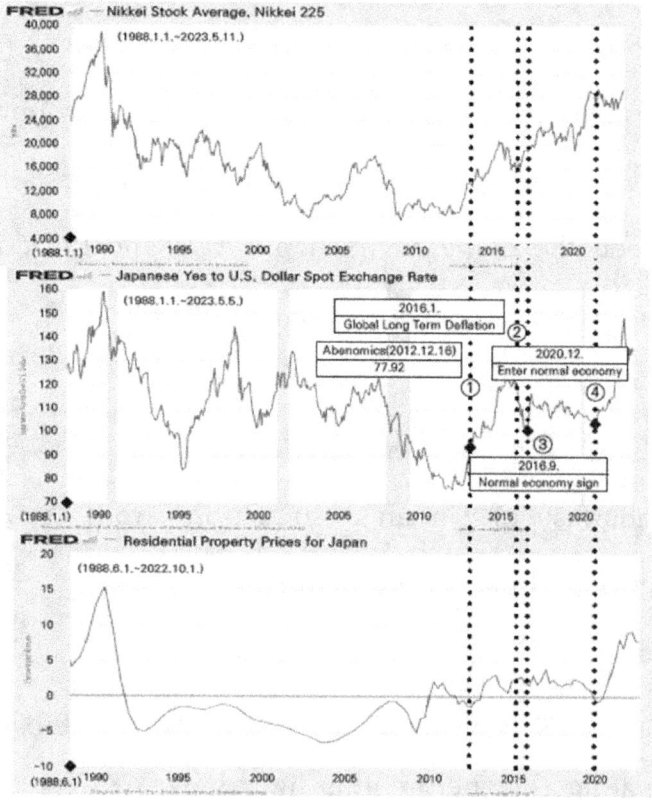

[Figure.27] Japanese Nikkei, Yen-Dollar, and Housing Index over 36 Years

This inverse relationship between the U.S. dollar exchange rate and the stock index indicates that the country's economy is in a state of short-term deflation according to the Diamond Dollar Investment Method.

After the vertical dotted lines BC'②, i.e. after December 1988, as the yen-dollar surges, the Nikkei also surges.
In other words, they start to move in a direct proportional relationship. This is the phenomenon of long-term deflation.

From this point on, after BC'②, we can say that the long-run deflation has occurred. If we look at the period between BB' and C', we can see that while the dollar surged by 30%, the Nikkei also surged by 29%, which means that the rate of increase is almost the same.

Let's take a closer look again. The vertical dotted line (A) in [Figure 2] and the vertical dotted line ① in [Figure 26] are the dates of Abe's inauguration as Prime Minister of Japan on December 16, 2020, when Abenomics began to be implemented.

In this time, we can see that the yen-US dollar exchange rate is rising, the Nikkei index is rising, and the Japanese housing index is rising. In other words, Japan was in a state of long term deflation at the start of Abenomics.

The vertical dotted line ② in [Figure 26] is January 2016, when Korea and the rest of the world entered long-run deflation. Vertical dotted line ③ in [Figure 26] is September 2016.

Let's take a look at the relationship between these two vertical lines, vertical dotted line ② and vertical dotted line ③. In other words, if you look between the vertical dotted line ② and the vertical dotted line ③, you can see that the Nikkei spikes when the yen-dollar exchange rate falls.

In other words, it is clear that in short-term deflation, the yen-dollar exchange rate and the Nikkei are always inversely related. In a long-run deflation, on the other hand, the relationship between the yen-dollar exchange rate and the Nikkei is directly proportional.

The relationship between the vertical dotted lines ① and ② in [Figure 26] shows that they are directly proportional.

In [Figure 26]①, i.e. January 2016, to the vertical dotted line ②, we can see that the yen-dollar exchange rate and the Nikkei index are directly proportional.

However, from the vertical dotted line ② to the vertical dotted line ③, the movement of the yen-dollar exchange rate and the Nikkei index became inversely proportional.

From ③ to ④, the relationship changes back to a direct relationship, and then to an inverse relationship. This means that from this point on, Japan is showing signs of escaping the long term deflation.

On the other hand, the rest of the world, excluding Japan, is in [Figure 13], indicating that the world has entered a long term deflation.

However, since December 2020 (vertical dotted line ④ in [Figure 26], the yen-dollar exchange rate has been rising sharply and the Nikkei has been falling sharply, i.e., the opposite is true.

Since December 2020, Japan's exit from a long-term deflationary state to a normal economy has been in full swing. This is the only evidence that Japan has been out of long-run deflation since December 2020.

The restoration of the inverse relationship between the yen-dollar exchange rate and the Nikkei index indicates the transition from a long term deflationary state to a short term deflationary state.

On September 22, 1985, the Plaza Accord forced the yen-dollar price from 240 yen to 140 yen. Until the yen-dollar exchange rate normalizes, the proportional and inverse relationship between the yen-dollar price, the Nikkei index, and the housing index will be repeated, but the long term deflation is over.

Abenomics has been successful.
The proof is after the vertical dotted line ④ in [Figure 26]. And the Nikkei 225 Index, 39,098 on February 22, 2024, is the proof.

This is the evidence of the success of Abenomics. Japan is now out of long term deflation.
According to the Diamond Dollar Investing Method, in a normal economy without long-term deflation, the yen-dollar price and the Nikkei index should move in

opposite directions and even have the same the rate of fluctuation.

This is not a perfect normalization, but the inverse relationship is clear. Since December 2020, Japan has moved from a long-term deflationary state to a short-term deflationary state, i.e. a normalized economy.

As shown in [Figure 26], the standard for determining whether an economy is in long-term deflation is the inverse relationship between the yen-dollar exchange rate and the Nikkei index, not necessarily the inverse relationship with the Japanese housing index.

In January 1990, Japan entered a long-run deflation in December 1988, precisely at line BC'② in [Figure 2].
No matter how hard it tried, there was no way out and no sign of it.

However, after eight years of quantitative easing by Abe, who took office on December 16, 2012, Japan's long term deflation should be considered resolved as of December 2020.

[Figure 26] is a graph showing the relationship between Japan's Nikkei index, the yen-dollar exchange rate, and the housing index over a 36-year period. The middle graph is the yen-dollar exchange rate and the top graph is the Nikkei index.

Both of these two graphics have a start date of January 1988. However, the housing index at the bottom has a start date of June 1, 1988.

The housing index in Japan is always five months behind the Yen-Dollar exchange rate, so the graph of the housing index has a start date of June 1, 1988 for easy comparison. Note that the start date for the Nikkei and the yen-dollar exchange rate is 1.1.1988.

I.e., if you draw a vertical dotted line anywhere on the graph [Figure 26], you can see the relationship between the housing index and the yen-dollar exchange rate on the same date and the Nikkei index on the same date.

Abenomics.
Abe said he would get Japan out of the high yen. With a 2% inflation target, unlimited monetary easing, and a negative interest rate policy, he has now succeeded.

On the other hand, Japan and the rest of the world have been sliding into long-term deflation for eight years already.

I believe that this process of fighting inflation has brought the world into a long-term deflation and a long recession. With the exception of Japan, the world may now be sliding into low growth and negative interest rates. On the other hand, the Japanese economy starts a virtuous cycle. First, yen that have been invested abroad will return home with their fruits.

The time has come for Japanese overseas investors to stop being ghost dollars and enjoy the fruits of their investment. It's time to buy Japan. No more "Japanese tears" or Japan's long term deflation. The 32-year period (December 1988 to December 2020) of Japanese tears is over.

It was recently reported that Mr. Big Investor has invested in Japan. He must be a savvy investor after all. It's time to invest in Japanese stocks because in any country, stocks move faster than apartments. Japan is a country where stocks start moving five months earlier than real estate.

For any country, it's important to research the order of investment in each asset and the time difference between investments.

Depending on the country's dependence on trade and the type of housing, it is normal for the timing to be slightly different. In South Korea, there is a six-month lag between investing in stocks and investing in apartments.

Japan's housing type is mainly single-family houses, while Korea's is mainly apartments. Korea's dependence on trade is about 70%, while Japan's is only 20%.

Common sense should tell us that Japan's housing index should move more slowly, but in reality, real estate starts moving five months after stocks in Japan and six months after stocks in Korea.

According to the original asset market cycle procyclical investment formula, i.e., the Pentagon Investment Method

1) The U.S. annual current account deficit is larger than the previous year,

2) Then, when a country's annualized balance of payments turns into a surplus a year ago, its stock index starts to rise immediately.

Then, after 5 months in Japan and 6 months in Korea, apartment prices start to rise. If you invest in apartments at this time, you will have bought at the optimal time.

This is the time to invest in stocks and apartments at the beginning of the new asset market upswing. These are the lowest prices for stocks and apartments, and you should always be careful not to miss them.

Depending on the trade dependency of each country, the

impact on the country's economy will be different, so depending on the trade dependency of each country, you should start investing in stocks first, and then, after a period of time, start investing in apartments.

Meanwhile, let's look at the present,
Starting in January 2016, after a long period of deflation, the author believes that Powell will make a "Powell mistake," like Volcker's mistake, by trying to cure inflation that has briefly returned.

That is, he will cut rates prematurely. The resurgent inflation will then need to be tamed with another couple of rapid rate hikes.

Interest rates are high now, too, but that means we could see high rates for quite some time. But after that, we believe the world will enter a true long-run deflation. In other words, the world may have to accept a period of high interest rates and 4-5% inflation.

The good news is that the world now has empirical data on how to fight deflation in the long run with Abenomics: massive monetary easing.

But that doesn't mean that the debt of households, businesses, and governments has been eliminated, and it doesn't mean that the problem of population decline has been solved, so I think we're going to end up with a society where the policy target of 2% inflation shouldn't be achieved. The world is destined for a high-interest rate, high-inflation world in the future.

In the meantime, Japanese people have not been buying stocks and houses in Japan as is customary. Stocks and apartments have been falling steadily for more than 30 years.

But now, to get rich, Japanese people have to buy Nikkei stocks, and they have to buy export conglomerates because it's the age of conglomerates again.

This fact will be missed by almost 100% of the Japanese

people.Historically, the yen-dollar exchange rate has favored mid-sized technology companies in Japan.But now, with the return of the high exchange rate, it's the turn of the export conglomerates.

In August 2022, Mr.Big Investor first bought $6 billion worth of shares in Japan's five largest general trading companies, the country's export powerhouses.Mr.Big Investor is increasing his investment further in 2023.Coincidence or research?

One of the two conditions for successful overseas investments is a strong local currency, and he knows that the Japanese yen is in the midst of a long cycle of weakness.

If the yen continues to weaken, foreign funds invested in Japan will suffer exchange losses when they return to their home countries.

If you invested in Japan by exchanging 110 yen for a dollar, and when you return home after selling your Japanese assets, the yen.dollar exchange rate is 150 yen, you will have an exchange loss of 40 yen per dollar.

Mr.Big Investor didn't invest in Japan by taking dollar funds from the U.S. to Japan, but by issuing yen-denominated bonds to Japanese commercial banks to buy stocks of Japan's five largest trading companies.

He borrowed money at an interest rate of about 0.5% or less and bought stocks of Japanese general trading companies with an average dividend yield of about 5%. He already had a 4.5% to 5% return on his investment.

We know some of the reasons, but we need to think about why? From his investment, we can get an idea of the future of Japan.

The Japanese yen hit a low of 76.34 yen to the dollar, and then went up to 151 yen in 2023. It is now around 150 yen. The author believes that the yen will be much cheaper in the future. The goal of the Abenomics policy is to lower the price of the yen.

If you want to invest abroad, you should go to a country where the local currency is stronger. Right now, Japan is printing money ad infinitum to lower the value of the yen. There are endless ways to weaken the yen.

However, it is an investment that assumes that the Japanese yen will strengthen again in the future, and when it does, foreign funds will once again rush to buy Japan as the yen strengthens, just like the Plaza Accord of September 1985. At that point, he would sell the rising stocks and buy dollars to get out of the Japanese market.

The fact that Mr.Big Investor began to invest in and significantly increase his holdings in Japan's five largest conglomerates, or trading companies, is also indirect evidence that Japan is out of long-term deflation.

Mr.Big Investor realized that these export-oriented conglomerates would profit greatly from the growing exchange rate differential.

The strategy is to earn an average dividend yield of about 5% per year for the duration of the holding period, and then, when the yen becomes expensive, buy dollars and return to the U.S. when the yen-dollar exchange rate is at its lowest, and thus keep all the dividends and exchange gains.

You should invest abroad when you can take advantage of capital gains and exchange rates. Investing abroad is like a hurdle race. The best time to invest abroad is after a stock, apartment, or government bond market crash in a country in the foreign.

I,e., the best time to buy a country's stocks, apartments, and government bonds is after the local dollar has skyrocketed and the local currency has crashed, and you'll be able to capture both the capital gains and the exchange rate gains.

One thing to consider is the recovery potential of the local dollar and how long it will take. I would advise most investors to avoid investing abroad.

But, in Japan, which is coming out of a long term deflation, the author strongly recommends buying export conglomerates due to the rising yen-dollar exchange rate.

Mr.Big Investor invested in shares of Japan's General Trading Company in anticipation of a stronger yen that would eventually return. It's the same reason why he sells yen-denominated bonds to Japanese banks to fund his Japanese stock purchases.

This method completely eliminates gains and losses due to exchange rate differences during the holding period.

It's time for Japanese people to start investing anew in Japanese apartments and other profitable real estate.

If they continue to invest in the same way they did during the long term deflation, they will be on a downward spiral again.

As the population of rural areas decreases, the demand for rural real estate decreases, so it is inevitable that rural real estate prices will fall.

However, there is no doubt that people will flock to real estate such as apartments in urban areas, so you should invest in apartments in urban areas.

The era of short-term deflation has now arrived in Japan.

I think Japan's long term deflation is over. This is thanks to Abenomics. Abenomics is a huge success. People should start investing in Japan now. Japan's tears, which have been secretly shed for 32 years (1988.12.-2020.12.), are over.

It is certain that all asset prices in Japan will rise. The yen is more likely to continue its decline. The era of the Diamond Dollar Investing method has finally been applied in Japan.

Therefore, I believe that the yen to won exchange rate below 700 won has arrived and the super cheap era is coming. Will there be a period of strength in the yen-dollar exchange rate in the near future, as predicted by Mr. Big Investor?

The author believes that the yen-dollar exchange rate should be judged by considering the exchange rate at the time of the Plaza Accord in 1985.

For 32 years, the yen-dollar exchange rate was super strong. From ¥260 to ¥78.6 to the dollar, it was 32 years of continuous yen strength.

Going forward, there will be an era of high interest rates

where the world will accept high inflation rates above 2%.
And it should be noted that since January 2016, the world, including South Korea, has been in a long-term deflation with household debt, corporate debt, and government debt,too.

This is when Japan seized the opportunity.However, Japan's government debt ratio is a whopping 248%. This is by far the highest in the member of the Organization for Economic Cooperation and Development.

The Japanese government cannot afford to choice fiscal policy liberally. Now that Japan has a chance to escape long-term deflation with a massive monetary easing program, it should choose a certain way to fully return to economic stability.

This is the sale of Japanese state-owned property.
At a time when real estate prices in Japan are rising, the government should sell off excess and unneeded state-owned assets to Japanese citizens and Japanese companies to pay off the government bonds it has already issued in a short period of time. This is the only way to turn the broken economy around.

Another way is to boost GDP. In the age of AI, dramatic productivity gains can reduce countries' debt ratios. However, the current stagnation in global economic growth is more due to a lack of demand than a lack of productive capacity, so this option has its limitations,too.

In any case, Japan needs to bring its debt ratio back to the average debt ratio of OECD countries. This will bring Japan out of the long-term deflation state once and for all.

In fact, it is the only way to get Japan out of a long-term deflation state. Keep in mind that all debt, whether it belong to personal, corporate, or government, does not go away until it is paid off.

Japan also should not forget that a persistent and excessive trade surplus is also a long-term deflation trigger, too.

Japan is a net creditor country, investing about twice its GDP abroad. This excessive overseas investment also reduces domestic consumption, which can be a source of long-term deflation, too.

Chapter 19)

When will the inflation economy come back?

When will we have another inflationary economy where all you have to do is buy stocks and apartments to get rich?

We've been talking about pessimism, now let's talk about hope.

Again, the timing of the exit from long term deflation varies slightly depending on the debt-to-income ratio of households and enterprises and demographic issues, depending on the trade dependence of each country.

In general, if the long term deflation progresses like Japan, the world will reach a normal economy only around 2016+32= 2048. We can compare Japan and South Korea to estimate the long term deflation period due to the difference in population problems.

As the population problem is different in each country, we can estimate the long term deflation healing period of each country. In Korea, the current situation is not applicable to the long term deflation process, but it is expected to end by 2029.
.
The reason
It is the result of analyzing the aging and aging process of the population, which has a great influence on the economy.

We can reason through these complex calculations, but it is obvious that unification is a way to solve the population and consumption problems at once,

First of all, it is important to be able to determine whether we have escaped long term deflation or not, i.e., whether the period for reverse divergent dollar investment has passed or not yet,

As I mentioned in the previous chapter, ⟨Famous Investor⟩ has been increasing its allocation to the stocks of Japan's five largest conglomerates since 2021, knowing that Japan has normalized its economy and that the biggest beneficiaries of the low yen are exporting enterprises.

In order to eliminate the exchange rate difference, he issued yen bonds to raise Japanese yen to invest in Japanese stocks. We don't know whether he's investing with theoretical knowledge or animal instinct, but his investment is timely. It's amazing.

Although the yen is low right now, if you know the status

of Japanese manufacturing, you are investing in the expectation that after a few years of normalization, it will return to the yen.

Now, after the period when the reverse Diamond Dollar Investment Method is applied, when the economy reaches a normal state where the Diamond Dollar Investment Method is applied as it is, we will be back in an inflationary economy.

"It's like relying on the natural healing power of the economy. Population and debt problems are not something that can be solved in a short period of time.

Meanwhile, Japan is a creditor country with about $3.5 trillion in foreign net financial assets (Korea's is $780 billion). Japanese funds invested abroad have been unable to return home due to exchange rate differences, but now, thanks to the cheap yen, they can return home in glorious gold.

For nearly 30 years, dollar funds have been floating around overseas financial markets. This phenomenon has given rise to the phrase "curse of the yen," and the Japanese yen has been treated as a safe haven asset. The yen is not a safe haven.

The simple fact is that Japan's long term deflation is still not fully healed. The yen has not returned to its normal exchange rate.

In a short term deflation, i.e., in a normal recession, the dollar price temporarily spikes along with the general decline in the stock market, but as we have seen, it returns to its normal value within a year or two.

It is also impossible to determine what level of dollar price is normal, so it is best to judge the normal application of the Diamond Dollar Investment Method.

If we look at Japan after 1989, which was directly connected from inflation to long term deflation, we can see that the dollar, which temporarily surged, continues to decline during the long term deflation.

Therefore, the techniques to recognize the beginning of a long term deflation and to recognize the end of a long term deflation are the most important "secret doors" to making a fortune. This is because the investment method is completely different for short term and long term deflation.

The rule of thumb is that economic agents will not have much room to increase consumption until debt reaches about 100% of GDP. After that, about 70 years of inflationary economies will begin again, and the 5 year boom + 5 year bust cycle will repeat itself.

It is expected that the long term deflation will continue until 2042-2043. In other words, it will be difficult to return to an inflationary economy until then. More precisely, it is the beginning of the long term deflationary economy where the diamond dollar investment method does not work.

Also, when the Diamond Dollar Investment Method works in reverse due to long term deflation, and then starts to work again, that is the time when the return to an inflationary economy is signaled.

This is when we will see a return to an inflationary economy after 70 years of inflation. Also, by this time, the fluctuating dollar prices of the countries mentioned in 1) ~ 4) will have returned to normal prices.

Therefore, it is much more accurate to check the relationship between the dollar and gold and the dollar and stock indexes from time to time to determine whether the Diamond Dollar Investment Method has reverted or not than a simple year forecast.

In other words, when the dollar and stock prices stop moving in the same direction and start moving in opposite directions, we have returned to the normal path, i.e., an inflationary economy.

This is the return to inflation we've been waiting for, and it's also the start of another 70 years of inflation.

Epilogue

About 90% of Americans invest in stocks. However, there are a lot of people in the U.S. who have never been near a stock market for the safety of their families.

That's 30 million people, or 10% of the US population of 340 million. The number of stock investors in South Korea is uncertain, but it is surprising that it is close to 10 million.

The author was born as a war child in a underdeveloped country and has learned, felt, and enjoyed many things while living in Korea, which has become a developed country.

After 50 years of being in and out of the stock and real estate markets, I became involved in South Korea's democratization process as a freshman in college. The school was closed every fall semester for almost four years. That's 50 turbulent years of learning and experience.

In addition, I worked as a TV producer at KBS for 30 years and experienced a lot of things. I started writing this book because I wanted to look back on my life and pass on my experiences to my children.

Korea has a very seniority-based work system, so there are people like this author who have 30 years of experience in each field. They don't seem to try to pass on their experiences.

I believe that people who have retired from their jobs, no matter what field they worked in, are the best experts in every field in the world. I think everyone has a responsibility to share their experiences with their children and future generations, because only then will our society become more and more advanced. Imagine a person who has been a janitor in a company for 30 years.

His 30 years of janitorial know-how can only be learned by someone who has worked for a similar company for the same 30 years or more. There would be a huge garage full of know-how on how to deal with visitors, how to deal with protesting shareholders, how to deal with fires, etc.

It takes 30 years for someone to master all of this know-how. But if you record his 30 years of experience, the next janitor will be able to learn from him in just one or two months and start working.

Korea has a rich heritage of documentation. Among them are 500 years of records from the Joseon Dynasty. To be precise, it is a royal history book that records 472 years of history from the first king of the Joseon Dynasty, Taejo, to the 25th king, Cheoljong, in chronological order, and is the world's best recorded culture, registered as National Treasure No. 151 and a UNESCO World Heritage Site in 1997.

No other country in the world has, or will ever have, such a long history of dynastic records. Currently, Korea has nine World Record Sites, while Japan has none. What's even more amazing is that our number of World Record Sites surpasses China's five. It is judged that we are the best cultural country in the world.

Our historical records have become World Record Sites because they are recognized for their objectivity, impartiality, and anonymity. Viewers should know that the scenes of the king and his subordinates standing alone in historical dramas are all fictionalized by TV stations for the sake of entertainment, and could never have happened at that time, i.e., if the king was alive.

The king would never meet with anyone alone without an official present. Also, the kings were not allowed to see the dynasty records, which is why they were recognized as a World Record Site. Our ancestors have such a brilliant recording culture, but for some reason, their descendants do not keep records, i.e. details.

♀Why they became such a non-record-keeping race is for scholars to study, but Li believes that anyone who works for 30 years in each job should leave behind the details of their field.
I've seen a book called "10 Years of Tropical Fish Farming" where Japanese people kept a diary of their tropical fish farming for 10 years by date and time.

I think Korea will probably never be able to catch up with Japan, which keeps records of these things, and the next person who grows the same tropical fish will become an expert immediately after reading this book. We Koreans don't keep good records anymore.

If a person grows tropical fish without reading this book, he will probably have to go through more than 10 years of trial and error before he can grow as many tropical fish as the person who reads this book without killing them.

We still haven't caught up to the 19-year gap between Japan's Meiji Restoration, which ended in 1877, and Korea's Gapo Gyeongjang in 1895. It seems that we are still several years behind Japan, an island nation that has always been hungry for our culture. To overcome this gap, we need to revitalize and develop our recording culture, which was once the most advanced in the world.

If you find it difficult to keep a record of your professional life yourself, you may be able to find a ghostwriter, either current or retired, who can turn your experiences into a book. In this way, I hope that retired professionals will actively pass on their valuable life experiences to future generations.

Publishing a book is not a difficult task these days. We have computers. It's not a manuscript culture anymore, so everyone who has been working in their field for 30 years or so should leave, leaving behind the details of their field. I strongly recommend that they leave with a foundation that will make Korea an advanced country among advanced countries.

If you are an expert, leave your details behind!
If anyone works or has worked in any field for 30 years,

he is the best expert in that field. If he worked as a shoe repairman for 30 years and managed a famous restaurant for 30 years, he is the best expert in his field.

If you're a lawyer and you've been doing civil or criminal defense work for 30 years, you've spent 30 years getting to the point of knowledge. This happens to architects, customs officers, oriental medicine practitioners, doctors, professors, and many other professions.

A friend once asked me why I write, if it's so hard to make a living from it. Of course, you can make a reasonable amount of money writing books. But I think the author should have 50 years of investing experience and 30 years of research to offer.

I think the author leaves a great legacy with the Pentagon investing method for stocks, apartments, dollars, deposits, and government bonds.

It is a method of rotating investment between asset markets that is so clear that anyone can get rich by following it. This book is a must-have for anyone who wants to learn how to invest.

The author doesn't know much about financial techniques or experience in investing in stocks, real estate, dollars, savings, government bonds, etc. except what he has written so far, so this is probably the end of his intellectual curiosity and writing for his children!

If you're a lawyer and you've been doing civil or criminal defense work for 30 years, you've spent 30 years getting to the point of knowledge. This happens to architects, customs officers, oriental medicine practitioners, doctors, professors, and many other professions.

A friend once asked me why I write, if it's so hard to make a living from it. Of course, you can make a reasonable amount of money writing books. But I think the author should have 50 years of investing experience and 30 years of research to offer.

I think the author leaves a great legacy with the Pentagon investing method for stocks, apartments, dollars, deposits, and government bonds.

It is a method of rotating investment between asset markets that is so clear that anyone can get rich by following it. This book is a must-have for anyone who wants to learn how to invest.

The author doesn't know much about financial techniques or experience in investing in stocks, real estate, dollars, savings, government bonds, etc. except what he has written so far, so this is probably the end of his intellectual curiosity and writing for his children!

The world is changing rapidly.
The AI era is opening up, the world of superconductors is opening up, and a world where robots replace humans is already here.

In order to ensure that our descendants in Korea can live as first-class citizens and survive, experts are leaving behind the details of the world they have experienced for more than 30 years!

In January 2018, the grandson who gave his grandfather courage when I was hesitant about publishing my first book, "The FinTech Secret Handbook only for My Children," said, "Don't worry, grandpa, be brave, it will work out, because no one is good at it from the beginning," is already in the second grade of middle school. His grandson, Hyunbae Son, was born in the meantime and will be in first grade next year.

Encouraged by my grandson's words, I started writing, and seven more books have been published since then. This book is the first book to study long term deflation in earnest in the world.

The author is not a celebrity, so sales are limited.
However, the contents of the book are all original, and the illustrations between the books are almost all drawn by his wife and daughter, i.e. 100% self-sufficient.

The author is proud to leave all the things he has experienced, known, and studied for future generations. I hope you will leave your own records.

2024.5.15.
At home in Pangyo, Korea

www.ingramcontent.com/pod-product-compliance
Lightning Source LLC
LaVergne TN
LVHW012248070526
838201LV00092B/161